Thomas
Cook

PARIS

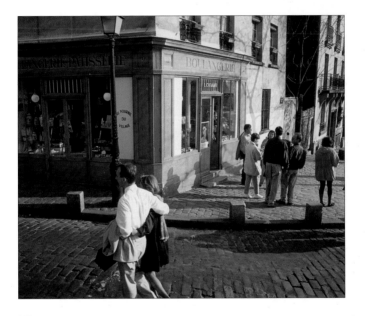

BY
ELISABETH MORRIS

Produced by
Thomas Cook Publishing

Written by Elisabeth Morris
Updated by Mike Gerrard
Original photography by Anthony Souter and
Ken Patterson

Editing and page layout by Cambridge
Publishing Management Ltd, Unit 2,
Burr Elm Court, Caldecote CB3 7NU
Series Editor: Karen Beaulah

Published by Thomas Cook Publishing
A division of Thomas Cook Tour Operations Ltd
Company Registration No. 1450464 England

PO Box 227, The Thomas Cook Business Park,
Unit 18, Coningsby Road, Peterborough PE3 8SB,
United Kingdom
E-mail: books@thomascook.com
www.thomascookpublishing.com

Tel: +44 (0)1733 416477

ISBN-13: 978-1-84157-703-6

Text © 2007 Thomas Cook Publishing
Maps © 2007 Thomas Cook Publishing
Métro map © 2007 Communicarta Ltd

First edition © 2002 Thomas Cook Publishing
Second edition © 2005 Thomas Cook Publishing
Third edition © 2007 Thomas Cook Publishing

Project Editor: Linda Bass
Production/DTP Editor: Steven Collins

Printed and bound in Italy by: Printer Trento

Cover design by: Liz Lyons Design, Oxford.
Front cover credits: Left © Jon Arnold Images; centre © David Noton Photography/Alamy;
right © Steve Lewis/Getty Images
Back cover credits: Left © Tibor Bognar/Alamy; centre © Ary Diesendruck/Getty Images

Contents

KEY TO MAPS

- ● M   Métro
- ☆   Start of walk/tour
- **14**   Arrondissement
- A100   Road number

Introduction

Fluctuat nec mergitur ('she is buffeted by the waves but she does not sink') has been the city's proud motto for more than four centuries … and still holds true today. Through revolutions, wars, foreign occupation and, above all, redevelopment, Paris has remained true to her image for generation after generation of enthusiastic admirers.

The sheer beauty of the capital conquers first-time visitors. A harmonious ensemble of splendid monuments and elegant domestic architecture provides a unique impression of unity; moreover, everything seems to be in its rightful place, from the Madeleine matching the National Assembly across the place de la Concorde to the unobtrusive place Dauphine at the tip of the Ile-de-la-Cité. Yet subtle planning and inspired improvisation are constantly remodelling the seemingly perfect image of Paris, and while pessimists predict that 'it will never be the same again', these innovations are being enthusiastically accepted by Parisians and outsiders alike. To give but three examples: the Eiffel Tower, which raised such an outcry when it was built

more than a hundred years ago, has become the most familiar landmark of the city; the controversial Centre Pompidou is now the most visited monument; and the Louvre would already seem incomplete without its pyramid.

However, beauty alone does not explain the attraction of Paris for so many. One could argue in favour of its vast cultural wealth, its *haute couture*, the infinite variety of its cuisine, or its reputation in the field of entertainment. However, its magical appeal is due mainly to an undefinable charm that seems to spring quite unexpectedly from the many facets of everyday life. Ordinary details, no matter how trivial, suddenly seem to acquire a new dimension: it could be a quaint-looking kiosk on a street corner; a whiteglobed street lamp in the middle of a tiny square; an old-fashioned shopfront; the *bouquinistes* (second-hand bookstalls) in the morning mist; or just an evocative street name like the rue du Chat-qui-Pêche (fishing cat street).

Full of contradictions, Paris never ceases to surprise: at once compact and spacious, it can be in turn pompous and modest, cheap and outrageously expensive, enthralling and infuriating, depending on the place and time of day.

'Nothing can be compared to Paris.'
From a popular 14th-century ballad by
EUSTACHE DESCAMPS

'This city without an equal, this summary of France.'
JEAN BERTAUT (16th century)

'Paris is well worth a Mass!'
HENRI IV, when he converted to Catholicism to become King of France

'Whoever looks into the depths of Paris gets dizzy. Nothing so fantastic, nothing so tragic, nothing so superb.'
VICTOR HUGO

'As an artist, a man has no home save in Paris.'
FRIEDRICH NIETZSCHE

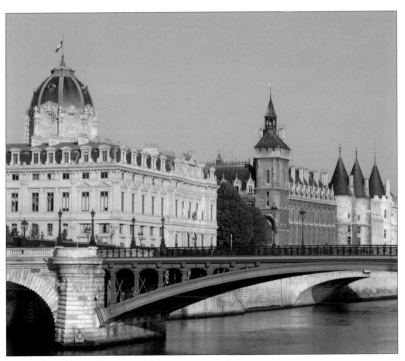

The Conciergerie, massive yet graceful

History

52 BC	Romans conquer the island; the settlement prospers and spreads to the left bank.
c.280	Barbarians raid city. The Parisii flee to the island.
c.360	Paris gets its name.
451	Attila's Huns attack. The young Geneviève predicts the town will be spared; she is later made the city's patron saint.
508	The first Christian king of the Franks, Clovis, makes Paris his capital.
7th century	King Dagobert is buried in the Basilica of Saint-Denis.
1163	Notre-Dame Cathedral begun by Maurice de Sully, Bishop of Paris.
1180	King Philippe-Auguste orders a new city wall and the Louvre fortress.
1215	The first university in France founded in Paris.
1253	The Sorbonne founded.
1364	Charles V starts a new wall around Paris and the Bastille.
1420	Height of the Hundred Years War: the English occupy Paris.
1430	Henry VI of England crowned king of France.
1436	Charles VII recaptures the city.
1546	New Renaissance palace at the Louvre begun.
1572	Saint-Bartholomew's Day massacre. Several thousand Huguenots die.
1578–1604	The Pont-Neuf is built.
Late 17th century	Louis XIV moves to Versailles, founds Les Invalides.
c.1760	Louis XV commissions the Ecole Militaire, the Panthéon and the place de la Concorde.
1789	The fall of the Bastille (14 July) marks the beginning of the French Revolution.
1792	Proclamation of the First Republic.
1793	Louis XVI guillotined. Louvre Museum opens.

1804	Napoleon is crowned Emperor in Notre-Dame.	**1940**	Paris bombed and occupied by Germans.
Early 19th century	The Arc de Triomphe is built, also theatres and shopping arcades.	**1944**	Paris is liberated.
		1958	Work starts on La Défense.
1848	Louis Napoleon, nephew of Napoleon I, elected first President of the Second Republic.	**1968**	'May Events' put barricades in the streets.
1852–70	Baron Haussmann remodels Paris.	**1977**	The first mayor of Paris since 1871 is elected and the Centre Pompidou is opened.
1870–71	Third Republic is proclaimed. The Paris Commune crushed at the expense of some of the town's finest monuments.	**1986**	The Orsay Museum and the Cité des Sciences are inaugurated.
		1996	Mitterand officially opens the Bibliothèque Nationale de France.
1889	Eiffel Tower built for the Exposition Universelle.	**1998**	France wins the football World Cup.
1900	First métro line opened. Paris becomes an international centre of fashion and entertainment. Montmartre witnesses the birth of modern art.	**2002**	Euro notes and coins enter circulation.
		2004	Celebrations are held to mark the centenary of the *Entente Cordiale* between Britain and France.
1914	Paris is saved from German invasion by the Battle of the Marne.	**2007**	France plays host to the Rugby World Cup, with the final being played in Paris at the Stade de France.
1937	The Palais de Chaillot and Tokyo built for the Exposition Universelle.		

The city

Paris is situated in northern France, at the centre of a vast natural chalk basin drained by the River Seine and its numerous tributaries, including the Marne and the Oise.

The Ile-de-France

The area surrounding Paris is, as its name suggests, the very 'heart' of France. This privilege goes back to the 6th century, when the region already formed the core of the kingdom of the Franks. Rich agricultural land, green valleys, beautiful forests, a temperate climate, easy communications and the presence of the capital in its centre secured its supremacy over the rest of the country.

However, the division of the whole French territory into some 90 *départements* at the end of the 18th century made the region's limits rather difficult to define. It was, for a long time, vaguely referred to as the 'Paris Region' and the name Ile-de-France seemed to be relegated to history books.

In 1976, France was divided into 22 regions, each including several *départements,* and Paris Region was officially given back its original name of Ile-de-France. The region comprises Paris and seven other *départements* clustering round the capital.

Since the introduction of gradual decentralisation over the past 20 years, the region has been governed by a Conseil Régional consisting of 197 councillors elected for a period of six years, assisted by a Comité Économique et Social, which advises on specific projects.

Economy

The Ile-de-France is an area of great economic wealth, modelled by its illustrious past but definitely looking to the future. It covers only 2.2 per cent of France, but accommodates a fifth of the population and has no fewer than five 'new towns'. It is by far the most densely populated of all the regions, and contributes more than a quarter of the gross national product.

THE TRUE PARISIAN

The population of Paris, like that of many large towns, has, with the influx of immigrants, become so cosmopolitan that the notion of a 'true Parisian' may seem like a myth. But visitors need have no fear: the true Parisian is still very real.

He or she may originally have come from a different part of France, or even from abroad, but once adopted by Paris, becomes a true Parisian: hurrying along the pavements and the métro corridors, hurrying to work and hurrying back home again in the evening, hurrying through life, in fact . . . not particularly amiable, especially if at the wheel of a car, but quick-witted and able to enjoy life intensely for a fleeting moment.

Nothing shocks or even surprises Parisians, and they would even be very tolerant . . . if there was time!

Commerce, transport and service industries are well developed, accounting for nearly three-quarters of the jobs. The industrial sector is almost as strong and produces a quarter of the total industrial wealth of the country. Power generation, electronics, publishing and printing, pharmaceutical products, environmental technology, information and communications technology, as well as food, are the main industries.

Agriculture, on the other hand, although far from negligible and highly efficient, is economically very much in the background and specialises more and more in the intensive production of cereals, flowers and ornamental plants.

The city

Neatly enclosed within a mostly efficient ring road, the périphérique (which can be very frustrating during the rush hour), Paris, dominated by the Seine, covers an area of a mere 105sq km (40^1/$_2$sq miles).

The population of the capital has now stabilised at just over 2 million inhabitants. During the past 15 years, the tendency has been for people to move out of Paris and settle in other *départements* of the region, which Parisians call *la banlieue* (suburbs). The areas surrounding the capital are officially referred to as *la petite couronne* (the close suburbs) and *la grande couronne* (the outskirts).

Parks provide havens of tranquillity for usually busy Parisians

Governance

Paris owes its unique economic and cultural drive to its long-standing role as capital of France. It took an active part in all the major events of French history, suffering greatly during the more sombre periods of revolution and war, but always recovering and regaining its vitality, wit and artistic taste.

Palais de Justice – its beauty belies its turbulent history

The corridors of power

Today, there are in France three distinct components of government: the parliament, the government and the president.

Parliament consists of two houses: the Assemblée Nationale, elected for five years, sits in the Palais Bourbon facing the place de la Concorde; it discusses and votes on the laws, while the Sénat, elected for nine years and housed in the Palais du Luxembourg, has a purely advisory role.

The government is made up of the prime minister, chosen by the president, and a variable number of ministers. Together they are answerable to the Assemblée Nationale for their policies. The prime minister resides in the Hôtel Matignon, in the Faubourg St-Germain.

The Président de la République is elected for seven years; he chooses the prime minister and presides over cabinet meetings. He is head of the armed forces, has considerable powers in foreign affairs, ensures the independence of the judiciary and may be granted special powers in exceptional circumstances. The Palais de l'Elysée is the president's official residence.

Helping to turn the wheels of power, the political parties and the trade unions are all based in the capital, as are the national newspapers.

Finally, one must not forget the people of Paris who have always shown great interest in the running of national affairs, and take an active part in decision-making through frequent street demonstrations and gatherings in public squares.

Embassies from countries all over the world have long been established in the capital, which is also the seat of major international organisations such as UNESCO (United Nations Educational, Scientific and Cultural Organisation) and OECD (Organisation for Economic Cooperation and Development).

Paris has lately become the most sought-after centre of international congress in the world, overtaking London and Brussels.

Town and département

At local government level, Paris has, since 1977, enjoyed the unique privilege of being at once a *commune* and a *département*. As a *commune* or municipality, it has an elected mayor chosen by the municipal council; elections are held every six years. The *commune* of Paris is divided into 20 *arrondissements*, each having its own mayor, and working closely with the central municipal authority, which meets at the Hôtel de Ville.

When the Ile-de-France region came into being, the Seine *département*, of which Paris was the main town, and several *départements* surrounding the capital were remodelled, and new ones created: with a fifth of the region's total population, Paris became a *département* in its own right, administered by the Conseil de Paris.

Decentralisation

The endowment on the local authority of real powers proved beneficial to the city as it enabled the municipality and the state to share the responsibility for the capital's great architectural heritage and to initiate daring futuristic projects aimed at maintaining Paris's position as one of the major modern European cities. Even if everything has not always gone smoothly, the results so far are stunning: whole districts, which had become derelict, have been restored (like the Marais), or completely rebuilt (like Les Halles), but their traditions have been preserved. At the same time, the renovation of eastern districts, neglected for far too long, was inspired by bold town planning principles with astonishing results: thus La Villette, in the northeast, is a major cultural attraction.

Excitement over the changing face of Paris is not about to abate, especially since communications and the environment have become very controversial issues in local politics.

The classically styled Assemblée Nationale, where the lawmaking body of the French parliament sits

Culture

Foreigners usually expect to discover in Paris the very essence of French culture and they are right to a certain extent, although provincial French people would not agree, however proud they may be of their capital. Wit, elegance and energy are all to be found in Paris. Parisians are aware that the rest of France is watching them and have always considered this a worthwhile challenge. As a result, they have developed a strong need to innovate, as well as a tremendous drive to achieve their goals.

Searching for rare editions from the *bouquiniste*

The changing face of Paris

A great deal of systematic restoration work has been undertaken, and a number of buildings have acquired a renewed and restored usefulness. The magnificent but obsolete Gare d'Orsay has been renovated in an imaginative way and turned into an art museum, while a glass pyramid lets daylight into the underground entrance hall of the Louvre Museum. The last of I M Pei's grand plan for this area was completed in 1999, at a cost of over $1 billion, making the Louvre the world's largest museum.

Moreover, for the first time, whole districts have been saved from dereliction with the help of modern techniques of conservation: in the Marais, for example, the splendour of the past has come to life again. At the same time, vast architectural projects initiated in the latter half of the 20th century ensured cultural continuity. Some of them, such as the Forum des Halles, La Villette and La Défense, are particularly striking.

A certain way of life

Parisians may be fond of new ideas, but they are also conservative, and their lifestyle reflects this constant conflict between innovation and tradition. Paris has always been a compact city and Parisians have become used to living in cramped conditions, in blocks of flats that traditionally have six storeys and a concierge (caretaker) on the ground floor. Therefore, street life is important to them: local bistros, brasseries and cafés are a favourite meeting place throughout the day. Open-air markets, where people from different generations and social backgrounds mingle in a colourful display of exuberance, have remained the focal point of many districts.

Furthermore, Parisians have a reputation for trendsetting: a district suddenly becomes fashionable and everyone wants to live in it. This phenomenon is also apparent in two other important aspects of Parisian life – clothing and food, where there is a definite cosmopolitan influence.

Subtle changes

The traditional way of life is gradually changing as the fabric of the population itself alters: the number of workers in high-tech industries, members of the professional classes, and artists is increasing rapidly, while the contrast between wealthy western districts and poorer eastern areas is disappearing. At the same time, the pace of living has considerably quickened, inevitably damaging personal contacts. On the other hand, Paris is becoming truly cosmopolitan, which has brought greater cultural variety to the Parisian scene.

Culture for everyone

Paris is as much as ever a melting pot of artistic creation and a place where one can never tire of being a spectator. Music, drama and the visual arts are taught at various levels, from the municipal schools to the national *conservatoires*.

Paris is also the place to visit for those who do not take an active part in culture but thrive on it. There are, of course, prestigious opera houses, concert halls and theatres, but there are also free concerts in many churches all over the city, and avant-garde plays in tiny, obscure theatres.

In addition to their permanent collections, museums and art galleries organise temporary exhibitions. The number of libraries is increasing rapidly, and there are still a record number of cinemas in spite of fierce competition from television. Also, this brief review of the cultural scene would be incomplete without a special mention of two great multipurpose cultural centres: the Pompidou Centre, and the music and science complex at La Villette.

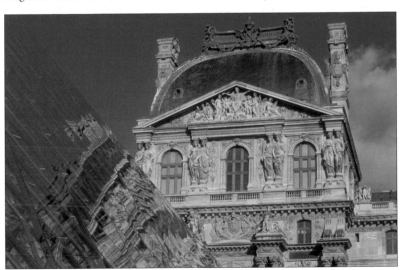

The stately 16th-century Louvre, now served by its glass-pyramid information centre

Festivals and events

Festivals stem from an ancient tradition, but their number has greatly increased in recent years and they have developed from spontaneous, regular gatherings into elaborate forms of entertainment aimed at occasional visitors as well as local residents. Below are some of the regular highlights.

Drumming up support in the Paris streets

IN PARIS
Jazz in the Parc Floral *May–July*
Bois de Vincennes.
Tel: 01 55 94 20 20.

Festival 'Foire St-Germain' *June–July*
Theatre, music, exhibitions and an antiques fair (St-Germain-des-Prés).
Tel: 01 43 29 61 04.

Festival Chopin *mid-June–mid-July*
Concerts and recitals. *Parc de Bagatelle, Bois de Boulogne, 75016.*
Tel: 01 45 00 22 19.

Paris, Quartier d'Eté *mid-July–mid-Aug*
Festival of popular entertainment, with venues spread across the capital.
Tel: 01 44 94 98 00.

Paris Plage *mid-July–mid-Aug*
The Right Bank quaysides of the Seine from pont Henri IV to quai des Tuileries are closed to traffic and transformed into mini-beaches, complete with sand, showers, sunbeds, palm trees and parasols.

Festival de Cinema en Plein Air
July & Aug
Tel: 01 40 03 75 75.

Festival Musique en l'Ile *July–Sept*
Classical music. *Eglise St-Louis-en-l'Ile, 19 bis rue St-Louis-en-l'Ile, 75004, métro: Pont-Marie; Left Bank, church of St-Germain-des-Prés, place St-Germain-des-Prés, 75006, métro: St-Germain-des-Prés.*
Tel: 01 44 62 00 55.

La Villette Jazz Festival *Sept*
Grand Hall, La Villette.
Tel: 08 03 30 63 06.

Festival d'Automne
mid-Sept–end Dec
Music, dance, plays and special exhibitions. *Tel: 01 53 45 17 17.*

Journée du Patrimoine *Sept*
A France-wide event where normally off-limits buildings such as the Palais d'Elysée are opened to the public.
www.jp.culture.fr

Festival d'Art Sacré de la Ville de Paris *end Nov–mid-Dec*
Church music at church venues.
Tel: 01 44 70 64 10.

Mois de la Photo *Biennial, even years*
Photographic exhibitions held throughout the city. *Tel: 01 44 78 75 00.*

IN ILE-DE-FRANCE
Contact the Comité Régional du
Tourisme d'Ile-de-France, *tel: 08 26 16
66 66,* for events in the Paris region.

Rueil-Malmaison *Jan*
Festival International du Film d'Histoire
devoted to historical films.

Abbaye de Royaumont
May, June, Sept & Oct
Concerts take place in abbey buildings.

Versailles *end May–end June*
Festival of instrumental music and
opera in the Opéra Royal at the château.

St-Denis *June*
A festival of music.

Fontainebleau *July & Aug*
Concerts are given in the castle.

Parc de Sceaux *July–Sept*
Saison Musicale d'Eté gives concerts in
the Orangerie.

St-Germain-en-Laye *Sept*
International music festival featuring
works by the composer Claude Debussy.

Suresnes *1st weekend Oct*
8km (5 miles) west of Paris, a wine
festival celebrates the harvests.

FAIRS AND SPECIAL EVENTS
Foire du Trône *Mar–May*
A funfair in the Bois de Vincennes.

Fête de la Musique *21 June*
In the 20 *arrondissements* of Paris.
Tel: 01 42 76 40 40.

Fête des Tuileries *July–mid-Aug & Dec*
Funfair in the Tuileries gardens.

La Fête Nationale *13 July*
A huge open-air ball on the place de la
Bastille, followed by a military parade
along the Champs Elysées on 14 July in
the morning and fireworks in the
evening at the Trocadéro.

Fête à Neu Neu *Sept*
Funfair in the Bois de Boulogne.

ART EXHIBITIONS
**Les Cinq Jours de l'Objet
Extraordinaire** *late May*
A display of antiques by dealers of the
Carré Rive Gauche, 75007.

**Foire Internationale d'Art
Contemporain** *end Oct*
Contemporary art at the Paris Expo-
Porte de Versailles. *Métro: Port de
Versailles or Balard. www.fiacparis.com*

Salon d'Automne *Nov*
Paintings, sculptures, photographs and
architecture. *L'Espace Charenton, 327 rue
de Charenton, 75012.*

Salon des Artistes Indépendants
Apr
Art exhibitions with different themes.
L'Espace Champerret, *Porte de
Champerret, 75017. Métro: Porte de
Charenton or Balard/Créteil.*

Paris Design Market *All year, every
Sun, 10am–7pm*
A meeting point for art lovers and
artists. *Boulevard Edgar-Quinet 59,
75104. Tel: 03 86 96 80 93.*

Impressions

'Paris is like an ocean; you can try to fathom it but you will never know its real depth.'
HONORÉ DE BALZAC

When to go
In summer Paris belongs to the tourists. If you are looking for authenticity, August is the worst month to visit, as the city is deserted by Parisians, cultural activities are at a low ebb, many restaurants and shops are closed and the weather can be uncomfortably humid.

Winter has a certain charm, with statues and monuments looking stark through the leafless trees, but the days are short.

Directional signage is clear and highly visible

Crowds in the streets reach their peak at Christmas time, a particularly lively period. January, with its traditional sales, is a good time for shopping.

However, late spring and early autumn are the most exciting seasons in which to visit Paris: in spring-time, parks and gardens are a haven of freshness, while the long warm evenings invite you to stroll along the Seine or watch the sun set, the Arc de Triomphe ablaze. There is a holiday spirit in the air which brings smiles and humour into everyday conversation.

Autumn marks the start of the return to the city – *la rentrée*, as the French call it. Restaurants, theatres and opera houses reopen, major exhibitions are announced, new trends in fashion are set, and children go back to school; moreover, Parisians are at their friendliest after their holidays spent away from the capital.

Getting around

On arrival, you might take a taxi and be whirled round the place Charles-de-Gaulle, which continues to be referred to as l'Etoile. This can be a hair-raising experience, but you will quickly come to terms with it when you realise that the *priorité à droite* (priority to vehicles coming from the right) really works – most of the time, anyway! From then on the pace is set, and you begin to get the feel of the place.

By car is definitely not the best way of exploring the French capital, both because of the large volume of traffic and the time restrictions on parking. Therefore, if you have travelled to France by car, your best course of action is to leave it in a long-term car park (ask your hotel for information on the nearest one) and take to the streets.

Walking is by far the best way to visit the centre as distances are manageable and there are no hills. However, sooner or later you will need to use some form of public transport. Paris is a densely populated, compact city, but careful planning has provided it with wide avenues and two main thoroughfares along the Seine.

Finding your bearings

Central Paris is relatively small and some of the familiar landmarks act as beacons: the Sacré-Coeur Basilica on top of Montmartre is due north, the Eiffel Tower is to the west, and the Montparnasse Tower dominates the southern part of town. Getting a detailed map should be your first move. All street signs show which *arrondissement* you are in, and if you look these up in the index of your Paris street plan, it will even give you the nearest métro.

Aerial view of the city

AREAS OF PARIS

The areas situated on either side of the Seine have acquired their own character, but there is a distinction dear to the heart of Parisians between the Right Bank on the north side and the Left Bank in the south. It goes back to the Middle Ages, when the growing city started to spread along the banks of the river.

The Rive Gauche, or Left Bank, became the students' headquarters and has since been the favourite haunt of a lively bohemian society. The Latin Quarter, St-Germain-des-Prés and Montparnasse have all been favoured by intellectuals at different times. Meanwhile, the Rive Droite, or Right Bank, traditionally conservative, has watched, sometimes with indulgence, sometimes with annoyance and even downright anger, the

antics going on across the river. A centre of business and commerce, it prides itself on having all the major department stores and *haute couture* boutiques (*see* Fashion, pp150–51).

Even Montmartre, at one time renowned as the poor artists' quarter, has acquired a definite respectability and been overrun by tourists, while the authenticity of the red-light district of Pigalle, at the bottom of the hill, has almost disappeared.

Where to go

You might find the following suggestions helpful when choosing a walk or an area to visit.

If you like medieval architecture and enchanting river settings, go to the Ile-de-la-Cité and the Ile St-Louis.

Arrondissements

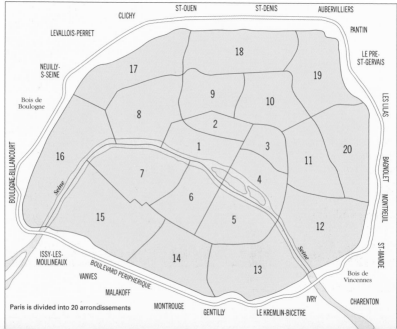

Paris is divided into 20 arrondissements

If you feel like taking it easy and mingling with a young crowd, aim for the Latin Quarter or St-Germain-des-Prés and watch the world go by from one of the lively cafés.

If you are feeling energetic enough to take on monumental Paris, walk up the Champs Elysées or experience the thrill of admiring the city from the top of the Eiffel Tower.

If you enjoy shopping in a grand way, the Madeleine/Opéra area is the ideal choice, but if you wish to meet trendy young people, then go to Les Halles and Beaubourg.

If discreet elegance appeals to you, and you enjoy going round the art galleries, the Marais is where you want to be.

If you like modern architecture, take the métro to La Villette or the RER (*see p20*) to La Défense.

And if a desire for La Bohème (bohemia) compels you to go to Montmartre, watch the artists at work on the Place du Tertre and then pause to admire the view from Sacré-Coeur.

Coping with the weather

On a rainy day, the main cultural centres like La Villette and the Centre National d'Art et de Culture Georges Pompidou offer varied activities for all ages, as well as meals and refreshments; so do the large shopping centres such as the Forum des Halles. Alternatively, the grand department stores in the boulevard Haussmann are so close to one another that you can go from one to the other without getting wet. Or why not take the opportunity to discover one of the lovely old shopping arcades located near the Palais-Royal, or stroll among the 250 boutiques of the Louvre des Antiquaires (*see p148*).

A melting pot of cuisine and culture

Public transport

The métro, the RER and the buses are part of a very efficient system. The métro, short for *métropolitain*, is a mostly underground network of 15 lines covering the city within the *périphérique*. Trains are frequent, stations are close to one another, and there is one flat fare throughout. You can either buy tickets in batches of 10 (a *carnet*) or get a *Paris-Visite* pass for unlimited travel anywhere for a specified number of days; you can combine it with a *Carte Musée-Monuments* (museum pass).

Maps of the whole network are posted outside stations and on platforms. You can change from one line to another at intersection points by following the sign *correspondance*. The métro runs daily from 5.30am to 12.30am; buses from 6.30am to either 8.30pm or 12.30am. Night buses (Noctambus) operate on 18 routes between 1am and 5.35am (*see p187* for more information on transport).

Travelling on the métro can be hectic, especially during the rush hour. A journey by bus is usually an enjoyable experience, but don't forget to allow extra time and to ring the bell when you want to get off. The same tickets are used on buses and on the métro, but you may need two on the bus depending on the length of your journey.

Route finders, which look like cash dispensers, are called SITU. They are programmed to work out the quickest way to any destination by one or several means of transport, including walking.

The RER (Réseau Express Régional) is a suburban network of fast trains linked to the métro. The flat-fare system applies only within the city boundaries. The RER is a favoured means of transport between Orly and Charles de Gaulle airport and the centre of Paris.

Within the Périphérique

Batobus

Riverbuses operate (*Apr–Sept*) between the Eiffel Tower and the Hôtel de Ville, stopping at the Musée d'Orsay, the Louvre, Notre-Dame and other spots.

Taxis

The best place to get one is from a *Tête de station* (taxi rank). Drivers accept a maximum of three or four passengers and expect a tip.

Paris Métro

A Communicarta
Style 45® design
© Communicarta Ltd 2006 UDN.7e
Map user Ref: WZFG/TVL/PAR/2006/49/4

SNCF
Versailles Rive Droite

SNCF
Bécon-Les-Bruyères

③ Pont de Levallois-Bécon

A1: St-Germain-en-Laye
A3: Cergy-le-Haut
A5: Poissy   RER

Grande Arche
de La Défense ①

Gabriel Péri

C1: Pontoise
C3: Argenteuil   RER

⑬ Saint-Denis
Université

D1: Orry La
Ville Coye   RER

④

Garibaldi

Porte de
Clignancourt

Mairie de Clichy

Porte de Clichy

Asnières-sur-Seine

Brochant

Clichy-Levallois

Simplon

Porte de St Ouen

Guy Môquet   Marcadet-Poissonniers

Jules Joffrin
Lamarck
Abbesses   Anvers
                   (Sacré Cœur)

Anatole France   La Fourche

Louise Michel   Blanche

Pont-Cardinet   Pigalle

Porte de   Place de Clichy   St Georges   Cadet
Champerret

Péreire-Levallois Péreire   Trinité   Notre-Dame-
                   (Maréchal Juin)   (d'Estienne d'Orves) de-Lorette   Le Peletier Gra
Pont de Neuilly   Boule
(Avenue de Madrid) Wagram   Rome   Chaussée d'Antin
Les Sablons   Malesherbes   (La Fayette)
(Jardin d'Acclimatation)   Villiers   Richelieu-
Porte Maillot   Monceau   Liège   Haussmann Drouot
Neuilly Porte Maillot   St-Lazare E
(Palais des Congrès) Courcelles   Europe   Opéra
                   Ternes   Quatre   Bo
Argentine   ⑭ Saint-Lazare Havre- Septembre
                                                    Caumartin
Charles de Gaulle   Auber
Étoile
           ⑥   George V   Miromesnil Saint   Madeleine   Pyram
Victor   (Souverain de   Augustin
Avenue Foch Hugo   Grande-Bretagne)
                                                                      Tuileries
Porte Dauphine   Kléber St Philippe- Champs-
(Maréchal de Lattre   du Roule   Élysées
de Tassigny)   Clémenceau
②   Boissière   Concorde   Palais-Roya
                           Franklin D.   Musée du Lou
Avenue Henri Martin   Roosevelt
                   Rue de la   Alma-Marceau Pont de   Musée d'Ors
                   Pompe   Iéna   l'Alma   Invalides
Boulainvilliers   Trocadéro   Champ de Mars-   Assemblée   Solférino
            La Muette Passy   Tour Eiffel   La Tour   Nationale   Rue du Ba
Ranelagh   open between   Maubourg
                                   (06.15 & 20.45)   Sèvres-
Jasmin   Avenue du   Varenne   Babylone
                   Président   Bir-Hakeim Dupleix   St François   Vaneau
                   Kennedy   (Grenelle)   Ecole Xavier
Michel Ange-   Avenue   Militaire   Duroc   Rennes
Auteuil Eglise d'Auteuil   Emile Zola
                   Javel Charles   La Motte-   Cambronne Ségur   Notre-Dam
                          Michels   Picquet-   des Cham
Michel Ange-   Mirabeau   Grenelle   Sèvres-
Molitor   Javel   Lecourbe Pasteur   Falguière
Boulogne   Chardon- André   Commerce
Pont de St Cloud   Lagache   Citroën
(Rhin et Danube)   Félix Faure   Montparnass
⑩   Exelmans   Boulevard Victor   Volontaires   Bienven

                                    Boucicaut   Vaugirard (Adolphe Chérioux)

⑨   C5: Versailles-Rive Gauche   Balard ⑧   Mairie d'Issy ⑫
Pont de Sèvres   (Palais de Versailles)
                   C7: St-Quentin-en-Yvelines RER

Arc de Triomphe

The Arc de Triomphe has, like the Eiffel Tower, a magnetic appeal for visitors from all over the world. This can, to a large extent, be explained by its exceptional situation at the top of a hill, almost halfway between the Louvre and La Défense. Its square outline, easily spotted from afar, is well defined against the sky by day and illuminated by night.

As much a symbol of France as the Eiffel Tower

Thirty years to build ...
Commissioned in 1806 by Napoleon as a tribute to his Grande Armée, it is the largest triumphal arch ever built in the pure tradition of Roman architecture. The design was that of architect Jean Chalgrin. However, work progressed slowly (it took two years to lay the foundations!). Chalgrin died in 1811, and the construction of the arch almost came to a halt after the fall of Napoleon. It was finally completed in 1836.

The arch today
In 1840, the hearse carrying Napoleon's remains passed, quite appropriately, under the arch on its way to Les Invalides. Then, in 1920, the Unknown Soldier was buried beneath it, under a plain slab, and, since 11 November 1923, a remembrance ceremony has been held every year.

The flame is rekindled every evening at 6.30pm. On special occasions, a huge flag floats beneath the arch to splendid effect.

Viewed from a distance
The arch is 50m (164ft) high, 45m (148ft) wide, and 22m (72ft) thick. Of the four sculptures on the façades, only the one by François Rude is famous. Known as La Marseillaise, it depicts the departure in 1792 of the volunteers, spurred on by a winged figure representing France.

Smaller reliefs on the façades and the sides feature victories won during the 1789 Revolution and the First Empire; a frieze by Rude and five other sculptors runs all round the arch. Along the top runs a row of shields inscribed with the names of victories won by Napoleon's Grande Armée.

GLORIOUS AND SOMBRE MOMENTS

In 1885, Victor Hugo, France's most popular man of letters, lay in state beneath the arch before being buried in the Panthéon.

On 14 July 1919, the allied armies celebrated victory by marching through the arch.

In 1940, the German army marched past it, greeted only by deadly silence.

In 1944, General de Gaulle was given a riotous welcome.

On 14 July 1989, the arch was the focal point of the joyous national celebrations for the bicentenary of the 1789 Revolution.

A closer view

A subway leads from the northern pavement of the Champs Elysées to the base of the arch. Underneath, the names of hundreds of generals are inscribed on the walls: those who died in action are underlined. It is worth climbing to the platform on top of the arch by means of the lift or stairs. The perfectly symmetrical place de l'Etoile and the 12 avenues radiating from it offer a stunning view. To the west is the vast modern complex of La Défense. The small museum houses an exhibition explaining the construction of the arch, as well as the main events connected with it; there is also a video show in French and English.

Place Charles-de-Gaulle

It used to be called place de l'Etoile because of its star shape, until it was renamed after General de Gaulle; but here tradition dies hard and l'Etoile it remains in the hearts of all Parisians even now.

Over 100 years ago, Haussmann remodelled it and built elegant neo-classical mansions all round. The 120-m (394-ft) wide avenue Foch is the most exclusive residential street in Paris; among its illustrious inhabitants were the Duke and Duchess of Windsor. *Tel: 01 55 37 73 77. Open: daily 10am–11pm (winter 10am–10.30pm). Admission charge. Métro: Charles-de-Gaulle-Etoile. Access by subway from the north side of the Champs Elysées.*

Nearby
Flower market on place des Ternes, FNAC hi-fi centre in avenue des Ternes, shopping arcades along the Champs Elysées.

The Arc de Triomphe floodlit at night

Walk: the Champs Elysées

This symbol of French elegance and glamour offers a unique and thrilling view that sweeps uphill to the Arc de Triomphe.

Allow 2 hours.

Start from place de la Concorde (métro Concorde).

1 Champs Elysées

The avenue was designed in the 17th century as a royal way leading out of Paris towards Versailles. Later, it became extremely fashionable to be seen driving along it in a horse-drawn carriage. In recent years, the Champs Elysées has been the scene of all major national celebrations, such as the bicentenary of the 1789 Revolution and, of course, the march past on 14 July.

Start walking along the main avenue.

2 Concorde to the Rond-Point

The paved avenue is lined with green open spaces planted with chestnut trees after the English fashion. The romantic alleys lead to half-concealed pavilions such as those occupied by the American Embassy and the Espace Cardin on the right-hand side.

Walk through the gardens on the left, and turn right along the Cours La Reine, then right again into avenue Winston Churchill.

3 Petit Palais

Like the Grand Palais facing it, the Petit Palais was built of stone and steel for the 1900 Exposition Universelle, and now houses the art collections of the city of Paris: Greek, Roman and Egyptian art; medieval and Renaissance objects, books and enamels; 16th- and 17th-century Dutch and Flemish paintings; 18th-century furniture and tapestries; and 19th-century French paintings by masters such as Delacroix and Cézanne. *Tel: 01 40 05 56 78.*

4 Grand Palais

In this imposing, glass-roofed building, adorned with an Ionic colonnade and elaborate sculptures, major art exhibitions are traditionally held, and the long queues winding outside this temple of culture are a familiar sight. At the back is the **Palais de la Découverte**, once a very popular science museum, but now overshadowed by the ultra-modern Cité des Sciences at La Villette. *3 ave. du General Eisenhower. Tel: 01 44 13 17 17. Open: 10am–8pm (10pm Wed). Closed Tue. Cross the Champs Elysées and continue along avenue de Marigny.*

5 Palais de l'Elysée

On your left, at the corner of the avenue Gabriel, a stamp market is held on Thursdays and Sundays. Further along on the right is the Palais de l'Elysée, built in 1718, which counts among its

Tomb of the Unknown Soldier, Arc de Triomphe

famous owners the Marquise de Pompadour and Napoleon's sister Caroline. Since 1873 it has been the official residence of the president. *Turn left into rue du Faubourg-St-Honoré, lined with shops, then left again into avenue Matignon.*

6 Rond-Point des Champs Elysées

Designed by Le Nôtre, it has an array of beautiful flowerbeds and fountains;

several of the surrounding buildings, such as the Théâtre Renaud-Barrault, date from the 19th century. The restaurant will provide a pleasant break. *Continue up the Champs Elysées.*

7 Rond-Point to the Arc de Triomphe

This section offers a marked contrast with the more pastoral lower section. Of the fashionable mansions built around 1860, only one has survived, No 25. It belonged to La Païva, an adventuress whose receptions were attended by writers and artists. The wide pavements teem with a cosmopolitan crowd attracted by the shopping arcades, cafés, restaurants, cinemas and big shops such as Virgin Megastore. On the quieter, south side is Fouquet's Restaurant, where celebrities come to be seen.

Nearby

Jardin des Tuileries, Musée de l'Orangerie, Madeleine, Musée Jacquemart-André, Avenue Montaigne, Palais de Tokyo, Musée Guimet, Théâtre des Champs Elysées.

Street café, Place de la
Bastille

Bastille

Even though all traces of the gruesome past disappeared long ago, the name Bastille is still charged with significance. In the minds of French people it has remained a symbol of the fight for freedom, commemorated every year on 14 July.

The Bastille fortress

Built in the 14th century as part of new fortifications to extend the city on the Right Bank, it was also intended as a residence for Charles V, who felt safe here. During the reign of Louis XIII it became the hated state prison and symbol of oppression.

The Bastille held some famous prisoners, including the Man in the Iron Mask, presumed to be Louis XIV's twin brother, the finance minister, Fouquet, and the philosopher, Voltaire. Shortly before the Revolution the prison was partially cleared and held only seven prisoners when the mob took it by storm on 14 July 1789. However, its fall unleashed the spirit of freedom throughout France.

Demolition began soon after. Some of the stones were used for the construction of the Pont de la Concorde, and within a year there was no trace of the massive fortress. On the first anniversary of the fall of the Bastille, people danced on the site.

The Place de la Bastille

The central column, called the Colonne de Juillet (July Column), commemorates the Parisians who died during the July 1830 Revolution. This lasted only three days, *les Trois Glorieuses*; the victims were buried underneath the monument, and their names carved on the shaft. At the top of the 50-m (164-ft) high column stands the elf-like figure of the *Génie de la Liberté*, the Spirit of Liberty. Paving stones follow the outline of the Bastille fortress on this otherwise ordinary square, which has become a traditional meeting place for demonstrations and celebrations.

The Opéra Bastille

In 1989, the fate of the whole district took a different turn with the opening of Paris's second opera house, which had already become a controversial issue in various Parisian circles. It was intended to be technically more modern, and created a new artistic centre in the less favoured eastern part of Paris. The Opéra Bastille, built by the young Canadian architect, Carlos Ott, was inaugurated on 13 July 1989, as a preamble to the celebrations for the bicentenary of the French Revolution.

In stark contrast to the ornate Opéra Garnier, the gently curved, sober façade of the building catches the faintest ray of sunlight, thus brightening up the surrounding area.

Tel: 08 36 69 78 68 for guided tours.

www.opera-de-paris.fr
Admission charge. Métro: Bastille.

The Bastille district

Traditionally occupied by craftsmen and small shopkeepers, the district had, by the end of the 1970s, become generally run-down. Following complete renovation, it shows every sign of becoming as chic and sought-after a place as its neighbour, the Marais. Art galleries, bars and fashionable nightclubs are to be found cheek by jowl with old-fashioned shops and dilapidated houses. The most colourful and liveliest streets are the rue de la Roquette and the rue de Lappe to the north of the square.

The Pavillon de l'Arsenal

Between the place de la Bastille and the Seine is the Port de Plaisance de Paris Arsenal, a new marina. To the southwest, at the end of the boulevard Henri IV, a museum, the Pavillon de l'Arsenal, illustrates architecture and town planning in Paris through the ages and new developments through changing temporary exhibitions.
21 boulevard Morland, 75004. Tel: 01 42 76 33 97. www.pavillon-arsenal.com. Open: Tue–Sat 10.30am–6.30pm, Sun 11am–7pm. Closed: Mon. Métro: Sully-Morland.

Nearby
The Marais, and Ile St-Louis.

Place de la Bastille: a bustling crossroads where a prison once stood

Ever since Paris was granted independent status in the 13th century, Parisians have never hesitated to rise against excessive political power, and the city has come to be considered as a very sensitive barometer of discontent.

The first major duel between the monarchy and the French people was fought and won in Paris in 1789. The signal was given when the crowd swept along the Faubourg St-Antoine to bring down the mighty Bastille on 14 July (still celebrated as a national holiday today). As a symbolic gesture, the Pont de la Concorde was later completed with stones from the hated prison, so that 'the people could forever trample the ruins of the old fortress'. Time and again, Parisians took the initiative, marching on Versailles to ask the king for bread, charging the Tuileries guards, listening to their leaders' fiery speeches in the Palais-Royal gardens, watching with gruesome curiosity as the rickety carts full of condemned prisoners jolted along the streets to the place of execution, or simply dancing and rejoicing on the Champ de Mars on the first anniversary of Bastille Day.

Scenes like these are vividly described in Dickens' *Tale of Two Cities*. King Louis XVI was executed by guillotine in the place de la Concorde (then the place de la Révolution) on 21 January 1793.

During the 19th century, the streets of Paris were set ablaze on several occasions by fierce fighting across hurriedly erected barricades. With the 1848 uprising, which began in the boulevard des Capucines, Paris did away with the monarchy for good. Yet in 1871, the Commune of Paris again challenged the government in a contest that ended in bloodshed in the Père-Lachaise cemetery. This time the Parisians lost.

A hundred years later, they showed that tradition could easily be revived when, in May 1968, students and workers barricaded the streets, bringing about General de Gaulle's resignation.

Left: Place de la Concorde; facing page: chaotic scenes in revolutionary Paris

Paris

Palais des Congrès

Porte des Ternes

BLVD PÉRIPHÉRIQUE

BLVD GOUVION ST-CYR

AVENUE DE WAGRAM

17

BOULEVARD DE COURCELLES

Parc de Monceau

BOULEVARD DES BATIGNOLLES

BOULEVARD

RUE D'AMSTERDAM

RUE DE CLICHY

St-Augustin

Musée Jacquemart André

Gare St-Lazare

RUE DE LA PEPINIÈRE

RUE ST-LAZARE

RUE DU HAVRE

Porte Maillot

AVENUE DE LA GRANDE ARMÉE

BOULEVARD

HAUSSMANN

Arc de Triomphe

AVE. DE FRIEDLAND

Lido

8

PLACE CHARLES DE GAULLE ETOILE

RUE TRONCHET

Opéra

AVENUE FOCH

VICTOR HUGO

Office du Tourisme

AVENUE DES CHAMPS ELYSÉES

Palais de l'Elysée

PLACE DE LA MADELEINE

Ste- Marie Madeleine

BLVD DES CAPUCINES

16

AVENUE

AVENUE D'IENA

AVENUE MARCEAU

Palais Galliera

Grand Palais

Palais de la Découverte

Petit Palais

RUE ROYALE

PLACE VENDOME

Jeu de Paume

St-Ro

Palais de Tokyo

Musée d'Art Moderne

COURS ALBERT 1 ER

COURS LA REINE

PLACE DE LA CONCORDE

Orangerie

RUE DE RIVOLI

Jardin des Tuileries

Palais de Chaillot

PONT DE L'ALMA

Seine

PONT DES INVALIDES

PONT ALEX III

QUAI DES TUILERIES

Jardins du Trocadéro

QUAI D'ORSAY

QUAI D'ORSAY

Musée Louvre

QUAI VOL

AVE. DU PRES. KENNEDY

PONT DE BIR-HAKEIM

QUAI

AVENUE DE NEW YORK

BRANLY

AVENUE BOSQUET

Esplanade des Invalides

QUAI ANATOLE FRANCE

Musée d'Orsay

RUE DU BAC

Tour Eiffel

PONT D'IENA

7

BLVD DE LA TOUR-MAUBOURG

Palais Bourbon-Assemblée Nationale

BOULEVARD ST-GERMAIN

Ecole des Beaux Art

Parc du Champ de Mars

Hôtel des Invalides

Musée Rodin

RUE DE VARENNE

BOULEVARD

QUAI DE GRENELLE

BOULEVARD DE GRENELLE

Ecole Militaire

AVE DE TOURVILLE

AVENUE DE LOWENDAL

BOULEVARD DES INVALIDES

Hôtel Matignon

RUE DE BABYLONE

RUE DE RENNES

6

UNESCO

AVE. DE BRETEUIL

AVENUE EMILE ZOLA

BLVD GARIBALDI

Jardin Luxemb

15

BLVD PASTEUR

BLVD RASPAIL

RUE LECOURBE

AVE DU MAINE

BOULEVARD DU MONTPARNASSE

BLVD DE VAUGIRARD

Tour Montparnasse

BLVD RASPAIL

RUE DE VAUGIRARD

Gare Montparnasse

14

Cimetière du Montparnasse

0 ½ 1km

0 ½mile

Bridges

Thirty-six bridges of greatly varying styles span the River Seine within Paris. Vital links between the Left and Right Banks, they open up large vistas across the city, thus directly contributing to its unity. Although some of them may have been rebuilt several times, their names often recall customs or events from various periods of the capital's history.

Gleam of gilt on the Pont Alexandre III

The Cité bridges
The Petit-Pont and the Pont Notre-Dame

In Roman times these were the only bridges crossing the river via the Ile-de-la-Cité. The Petit-Pont, so-called because it is the smaller of the two, was first built of stone when the construction of Notre-Dame was undertaken, but periodic floods have taken their toll, and it has been rebuilt 11 times. The present bridge dates from 1853. The Pont Notre-Dame, overladen with richly decorated houses, also had to be rebuilt several times. The present one dates from 1913.
Métro: St-Michel or Cité.

The Pont au Change

Although built between 1858–60, this bridge has a medieval name, a reminder of the days when the houses and shops built on it belonged to moneychangers.
Métro: Châtelet.

The Pont au Double

This bridge, linking the Left Bank and the island, acquired its strange name in the Middle Ages because the toll imposed at that time was a coin named a *double*.
Métro: St-Michel.

The Pont-Neuf

Curiously enough, this is the oldest bridge in Paris, built in the 16th century. Situated at the tip of the Ile-de-la-Cité, it offers exceptional views downriver. It was never built on, a great novelty at the time, but the carvings that decorate it illustrate 'dentists' busily pulling teeth, entertainers, and assorted stalls, which were all part of the daily scene 400 years ago. The two halves, which are not in line, are separated by the place du Pont-Neuf, where there is an equestrian statue of King Henri IV. Although it has been restored many times, the bridge remains unchanged to this day.
Métro: Pont-Neuf.

The Pont Alexandre III

Built for the 1900 Exposition Universelle, this bridge provides a link between the classical architecture of Les Invalides and the pompous steel and glass style of the Grand Palais. Each end is adorned with two allegorical sculptures, featuring medieval France and

modern France on the Left Bank side, Renaissance France and France under Louis XIV on the Right Bank side.
Métro: Invalides.

The Pont de l'Alma
The original bridge, built in 1854 to commemorate a Franco-British victory during the Crimean War, had to be replaced 20 years ago because the supports were sinking. However, the Zouave soldier beneath it, who indicates the level of the river, was preserved.
Métro: Alma-Marceau, Pont de L'Alma.

The Pont des Arts
The city's first pedestrian iron bridge is a romantic structure dating from 1803.
Métro: Pont-Neuf.

The Pont de la Concorde
Begun in 1788 by the civil engineer, Jean Rodolphe Perronnet, it was only completed after the fall of the Bastille. Since then, it has reflected many political upheavals by changing its name every time something significant happens. In 1830, the name Concorde was definitely adopted for good.
Métro: Assemblée Nationale.

The Pont-Royal
This bridge epitomises the discreet elegance that is one of the most attractive features of Paris. It was built by Jacques Gabriel during the reign of Louis XIV – hence its royal name.
Métro: Rue du Bac.

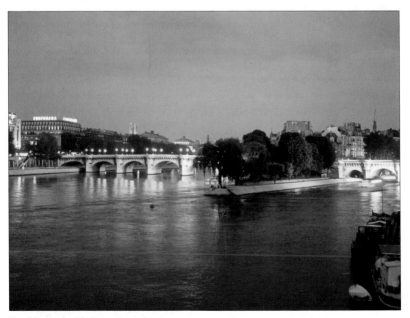

The Pont-Neuf, with 12 varying arches

Centre Georges Pompidou

Its full name – Centre National d'Art et de Culture Georges Pompidou – gives a fair idea of the vast scope of this multi-purpose cultural centre, and explains its enormous popularity, in spite of the controversy that is still going on about its design more than 20 years after its inauguration.

Art can be found outside the centre, too

Beaubourg

After the removal of the old food market in 1968, the Beaubourg area was included in the huge town-planning programme centred round Les Halles. President Pompidou then decided to build a multipurpose centre for modern and contemporary art on the site (*see* Walk *pp38–9*).

A futuristic design

Two young architects, Richard Rogers (British) and Renzo Piano (Italian), designed the complex, which was inaugurated in 1977, three years after President Pompidou's death. To some people it looks like an oil refinery or even scaffolding on a building site, while others, with a more optimistic outlook, see it as a contemporary piece of sculpture. In order to have as much free space as possible inside, lifts, stairs, escalators and ventilation shafts were fitted on the outside, hence its cluttered appearance.

There is a public information library with French and foreign books, slides and films; an industrial design centre featuring architecture, town planning and industrial design; an acoustics and music research centre for the purpose of sound experimentation; a children's workshop; a cinema; an assortment of rooms for temporary exhibitions, concerts and lectures; and, of course, the Musée National d'Art Moderne.

A *laissez-passer d'une journée* (day pass) will enable you to see all the exhibitions and to visit the museum.

Musée National d'Art Moderne

This is situated on the third and fourth floors; the entrance is on the fourth floor, which you can reach via the serpent-like escalator accessible from the main hall.

The collections of the former Musée d'Art Moderne, retracing the evolution of art through the 20th century, were transferred from the Palais de Tokyo and have since been considerably extended to include contemporary art.

The third floor houses frequently renewed exhibits of abstract and figurative contemporary art from 1965 onwards, while the fourth floor displays all the major currents of modern art from 1905 to 1965. On this floor there are two main sections: on the south (St-Merri) side as you enter, you can see the early 20th-century trends – Fauvism and Cubism – while on the north side the main post-World War I trends are represented.

The south side

The striking colours characteristic of Fauvism are illustrated in works by Derain, Vlaminck and, above all, Matisse, while Bonnard, whose work does not fit into the main trends, is also well represented.

There is a large selection of works by the main exponents of Cubism: Braque, Picasso, Gris and also Léger.

The north side

Abstract art is represented by Mondrian, Kupka, Klee and Delaunay. The sombre, mystic style of Rouault and Chagall's world of fantasy dominate the 1920s and 1930s, alongside the Dada movement, which deliberately derided society.

Surrealism is well represented by Dalí, Magritte, Ernst, Miró and Masson; so is the Cobra Group headed by Asger Jorn after World War II. The American school of Abstract Expressionism is strikingly represented by Pollock's 'drip-and-splash' style. The 1960s saw the advent of New Realism, and Pop Art flourished with Andy Warhol.

The fifth floor offers you a chance to relax in the pleasant cafeteria and enjoy beautiful views over the capital.
Place Georges Pompidou, 75004.
Tel: 01 44 78 12 33.
www.centrepompidou.fr.
Open: daily 11am–10pm. Closed: Tue.
Admission charge. Métro: Rambuteau,
Châtelet & Hôtel de Ville.

Pompidou Centre: something for everyone

Walk: Beaubourg and Les Halles

Major redevelopment gave this district a new lease of life in the 1970s, and today the area attracts a crowd of young trendsetters, while the gastronomic tradition has been maintained by the score of small restaurants that once surrounded the old food market.

Allow 2 hours (excluding visit to Georges Pompidou Centre).

Coming out of the Hôtel de Ville métro station, follow avenue Victoria and turn right into rue St-Martin.

1 Tour St-Jacques

The Tour St-Jacques on the left is all that remains of the 16th-century church of

St-Jacques-de-la-Boucherie, a starting point for pilgrims bound for Santiago de Compostela. Nearby there is a statue of Pascal, who conducted barometric experiments in the tower.
Continue along rue St-Martin.

2 Around St-Merri

The names of the streets surrounding the late-Gothic church of St-Merri recall their association with medieval trades. There is rue de la Verrerie (glassmakers) alongside the church and, opposite, rue des Lombards, named after the family who set themselves up as moneylenders. The rue St-Martin is lined with shops and bistros. On the north side of the church, the intrusion of the 20th century is emphasised by the colourful fountain in the middle of the place Igor-Stravinsky.
Just north of the place is the Centre Georges Pompidou (see pp36–7).

3 Centre Pompidou

Although used to designate the Centre Pompidou, Beaubourg is the name of the old district that has come into the limelight following the success of the cultural centre. North of the Centre lies the Quartier de l'Horloge: a lively pedestrian area of narrow streets and arcades, with numerous shops and a curious modern clock, called Le Défenseur du Temps (the Defender of Time), in rue Bernard-de-Clairvaux.
Return to the place Igor-Stravinsky and turn right into the rue Aubry-le-Boucher.

4 Les Halles

Rest awhile in the square des Innocents: it has the most beautiful Renaissance fountain. The neat gardens have replaced the old food market – gone underground. Escalators lead down into the Forum, a multi-level entertainment and shopping centre (*see pp54–5).*
Come up on the rue Rambuteau side and walk to the church of St-Eustache (see p40), then round it for the best views.

5 Bourse du Commerce

As you leave rue du Jour, you can see the Bourse du Commerce in front of you; it replaced the city's corn exchange in 1889. To the right is rue Coquillière, lined with restaurants, including the famous Au Pied de Cochon. Halfway down rue Jean-Jacques-Rousseau on the right is the charming Galerie Véro-Dodat with its quaint shops.
At the end of the street, turn left into rue St-Honoré.

6 Oratoire du Louvre

The 17th-century church by Le Mercier was used as the royal chapel under Louis XIII, Louis XIV and Louis XV, who listened to the sermons of famous preachers such as Bossuet. After the revolution of 1789, it became a Protestant church.
Turn right into rue du Louvre to reach the embankment; the church of St-Germain-l'Auxerrois (see p41) offers an interesting mixture of styles. Admire the lovely view of the Conciergerie from the quai de la Mégisserie. The place du Châtelet, where you can take the métro, has an impressive fountain in the middle.

Nearby
Palais du Louvre, Théâtre de la Ville.

Churches

St-Eustache: imposing inside and out

St-Etienne-du-Mont

Begun in 1492, the church was only completed in 1626. Its originality lies in its harmonious combination of styles: the chancel and the tower are late Gothic, and the Renaissance façade is unique with its three superimposed pediments. Inside, the church is well lit by a row of windows replacing the traditional triforium. The magnificent rood screen, framed by two graceful open spiral staircases, was built at the beginning of the 16th century by Antoine Beaucorps according to drawings by Philibert Delorme. Notice the beautiful pulpit, dating from 1650, and the attractive 16th-century stained glass behind it. Past the rood screen on the right is St Geneviève's shrine, containing relics of the patron saint of Paris. Philosopher and mathematician, Pascal, and the playwright, Racine, are buried behind the chancel.

1 Place Ste-Geneviève, 75005, behind the Panthéon. Open: Tue–Fri 8.45am–7.30pm, Sat 8.45am–12.45pm & 2–7.45pm, Sun 8.45am–12.15pm & 2.30–7.45pm. Mon: noon–7.30pm. Métro: Cardinal-Lemoine.

St-Eustache

This was the parish church of Les Halles, and now that the old food market has gone, it can be seen from afar. In 1532 work started on an imposing Gothic building modelled on Notre-Dame and dedicated to St Eustace. Although it took over 100 years to build, the original plans were followed to the letter, and it was a truly Gothic church that was consecrated in 1637. Unfortunately, the 18th-century neoclassical façade that replaced the original one has rather spoilt the overall effect. Many famous people are connected with St-Eustache: Richelieu and Molière were baptised within its walls; the latter was also buried there, as were the author, La Fontaine, Colbert, Louis XIV's finance minister, and the composer, Rameau. The dimensions of the building are even more impressive from the inside than the outside. Notice the unusual height of the double aisles, the fine vault, and the stained-glass windows in the chancel, dating from 1631 and featuring St Eustace among the apostles. The church is decorated with exceptional monuments and fine works of art, including *Les Pèlerins d'Emmaüs*, an early Rubens; it also has a strong musical tradition.

Place du Jour, 75001, next to the Forum des Halles. Métro: Les Halles. Open: 9am–7.30pm.

St-Germain-des-Prés

This was the church of a powerful Benedictine abbey, a great centre of learning, which owned most of the Left Bank until the 17th century. The abbey buildings were destroyed during the 1789 Revolution, but the Romanesque church was saved and restored in the 19th century. It offers an original mixture of styles: the chancel and nave are Romanesque with Gothic vaulting, the massive tower acquired a steeple in the 19th century, and the original porch is masked by a door added in 1607. Inside, the chancel and ambulatory are the most interesting parts: notice the traditional carvings on the capitals and the ornamental triforium; the marble shafts of its columns come from the original 6th-century church.

Place St-Germain-des-Prés, 75006. Métro: St-Germain-des-Prés. Open: Mon–Sat 8am–7.45pm, Sun 9am–8pm.

St-Germain-l'Auxerrois

The church was built in the 12th century, but has been continually remodelled for 400 years. As a result, it has a Romanesque belfry, a Gothic chancel and a late-Gothic porch, while the aisle round the chancel is Renaissance. It is unfortunately associated with one of the darkest episodes of French history. In 1572, its bells gave the signal for the Massacre of St Bartholomew when thousands of Protestants were murdered as a result of a plot between the Cardinal, Duc de Guise, Catherine de Médicis, Charles IX and the future Henri III. Inside, there are some interesting works of art, including a 16th-century Flemish reredos in the fourth chapel on the left of the nave, 15th-century stained glass in the transept and the rose windows, and a polychrome statue of St-Germain in front of the chancel.

Place du Louvre, 75001. Métro: Louvre. Open: 8am–7pm.

Other churches
Eglise du Dôme des Invalides (see p57).
La Madeleine (see pp104–5).
Notre-Dame (see pp92–3).
Notre-Dame-des-Blancs-Manteaux (see p73).
Notre-Dame-des-Victoires (see p97).
Oratoire du Louvre (see p39).
Sacré-Coeur (see p100).

Stunning window, St-Germain-l'Auxerrois

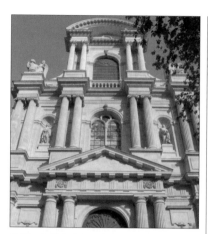
St-Gervais-St-Protais

St-Gervais-St-Protais

Dedicated to two Roman officers martyred under Nero, this church offers an interesting contrast of styles: the main part is late Gothic with a three-tiered classical façade. Inside, there are beautifully carved stalls, 16th- and 17th-century stained glass, and a fine 17th-century organ.

Place St-Gervais, 75004. Métro: Hôtel de Ville. Open: Mon–Fri 6am–9pm, Sat–Sun 7am–9pm.

St-Medard

This late Gothic church was completed in the 17th century. Inside, there is a 16th-century triptych, as well as other paintings of the French school and an interesting 17th-century organ loft.

Rue Mouffetard, 75005. Closed: Mon. Métro: Censier-Daubenton.

St-Merri

This is another late Gothic church, completed in 1612. The interior was considerably remodelled under Louis XV, and the only original features are the stained-glass windows in the chancel.

The composer, Camille Saint-Saëns, used to play on the 17th-century organ, and there are regular concerts in the summer.

Rue de la Verrerie, 75004. Métro: Hôtel de Ville or Châtelet. Open: daily 3–5pm.

St-Roch

St-Roch is a fine example of classical architecture. Its foundation stone was laid by Louis XIV in 1653, but work was delayed through lack of funds and it was not completed until the 18th century. The façade, which is in the Jesuit style, dates from 1735. In 1795, Bonaparte charged a group of royalist rebels here. The bullet holes can still be seen on the façade.

Rue St-Honoré, 75001. Closed: Sun except between 5–6.30pm. Métro: Pyramides or Tuileries.

St-Séverin

Situated in one of the oldest districts of Paris, St-Séverin is named after a hermit who lived in the area in the 6th century. Work on the present building began in the 13th century, and went on until

The Butte St-Roch

The church of St-Roch was originally built on a hillock upon which stood several windmills. The butte was levelled off as part of Baron Haussmann's ambitious town-planning programme, and the windmills all disappeared, except one, the Moulin Radet. This was removed to another high position, the Butte Montmartre, where you can still see it, in rue Lepic.

1530. Thus, the façade and part of the nave are basically early Gothic, while the rest is late Gothic.

In 1681, the Grande Mademoiselle, Louis XIV's cousin, had the chancel altered by the famous architect, Le Brun. The 13th-century west door originally belonged to a nearby church that was demolished in 1839. Inside, the most remarkable feature is the double ambulatory, with its spiral central columns looking like palm trees under the ribbed vaulting. There is beautiful 16th-century stained glass in the upper windows, and modern stained glass by Bazaine in the chapels at the east end. *Rue des Prêtres-St-Séverin, 75005. Open: Mon–Sat 11am–7.30pm, Sun 9am–10.30pm. Métro: St-Michel or Cluny-La Sorbonne.*

St-Sulpice

The church was originally built by the Abbey of St-Germain-des-Prés as a parish church for the surrounding area. The present building was started in 1646, and many architects worked on it until 1732, when it was decided to abandon the austere classical style. The Florentine architect, Servandoni, was selected to give the church an Italian-style façade.

Notice two giant shells mounted on supports carved by Pigalle as you enter; they were offered by the Venetian Republic in 1745. The first chapel on the right as you face the chancel has remarkable murals full of romantic inspiration, painted by Delacroix between 1849 and 1861.
Place St-Sulpice, 75006, near the Luxembourg gardens and St-Germain-des-Prés. Métro: St-Sulpice. Open: 7.30am–7.30pm. The Musée National Delacroix is nearby.

St-Julien-le-Pauvre (see p61).
St-Louis-des-Invalides (see p57).
St-Louis-en-l'Ile (see p47).
St-Nicolas-du-Chardonnet (see p62).
St-Paul-St-Louis (see p71).
St-Pierre-de-Montmartre (see p75).
St-Thomas-d'Aquin (see p103).
Ste-Chapelle (see pp100–101).

The classical façade of St-Roch

Ile-de-la-Cité

It is no coincidence that the history of Paris began on this small, boat-shaped island in the middle of the Seine. Although the river has lost its once essential role, this tiny strip of land, known as the Ile-de-la-Cité, has remained the heart of the great metropolis that developed around it.

The Conciergerie illuminated

Lutetia

This was the name given to the city by the first known settlers, the Parisii: it was a Celtic word meaning 'a dwelling surrounded by water'.

The 'Cité'

The Romans brought organisation and prosperity, but after the fall of the Roman Empire, the small island was in peril once again. Although it miraculously escaped the Huns, the Franks besieged it and eventually conquered it. When King Clovis made it his capital in 508, it became known as the 'Cité'. Its renewed prosperity attracted attention and it was soon threatened by Norman raids. The city was sacked several times until Eudes, Count of Paris, reinforced its fortifications and successfully defended it in 885. For more than 100 years afterwards, however, the town remained within the perimeter of the island.

The role of the cathedral

As a centre of learning, the cathedral played an essential role in maintaining the influence of the Cité after the town began to spread along the banks of the river. Schools flourished between the north side of Notre-Dame and the Seine, an area that belonged to the canons of the cathedral. Abélard was among the many students drawn to the Cité by the reputation of its teaching, and it was in the cloister school that he first met Héloïse (*see p60*). By the end of the 13th century, there were 22 chapels and churches near the cathedral.

The Supreme Court

From the 14th century onwards, the kings of France ceased to live in the Cité, preferring the Louvre and other royal residences outside Paris. The royal palace became the seat of the Supreme Court of Justice. During the Terror, the dreaded *Tribunal révolutionnaire* held its sessions there, next door to the notorious Conciergerie.

A quiet revolution

The island has changed considerably since the Middle Ages, but its most spectacular remodelling took place during the second half of the 19th century. It was during that time that the area round the cathedral was cleared and began to look as it does today.

The Palais de Justice

This part of the old royal palace, many times destroyed by fire, and considerably

extended in the 19th century, has completely lost its medieval aspect, but it is still worth walking across the main courtyard to the bustling Galerie Marchande, before visiting the Ste-Chapelle and the Conciergerie.
Ste-Chapelle, 4 boulevard du Palais, 75001. Open: 10am–5pm.

The Conciergerie

This is the oldest part of the former royal palace, bordering the Seine along the quai de l'Horloge. It gets its name from the *concierge* (caretaker) who looked after the royal residence and was allowed to levy taxes. The building already served as a prison before the Revolution, and during the Terror it held such famous prisoners as Marie Antoinette and Danton. Guided tours take you through the Salle des Gardes and the impressive Salle des Gens d'Armes with superb Gothic vaulting to the vast kitchens, the Galerie des Prisonniers and Marie Antoinette's cell.
Conciergerie, 2 bd du Palais, 75001. Tel: 01 53 40 60 97. Open: daily 9.30am–6pm. Admission charge. Métro: Cité.

Nearby
Ile St-Louis (*see pp46–7*); churches of St-Séverin and St-Julien-le-Pauvre; picturesque streets: place St-Michel; **Ste-Chapelle** (*see pp100–101*); **Cluny museum** (*see p61*); **Notre-Dame Cathedral** (*see pp92–3*).

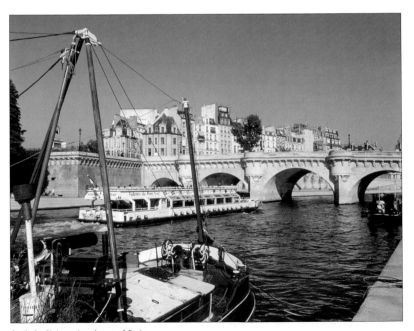

Ile-de-la-Cité, ancient heart of Paris

Walk: the Ile-de-la-Cité and Ile St-Louis

This is the heart of medieval Paris: the bustling Ile-de-la-Cité with Notre-Dame Cathedral solidly camped at its eastern end and, next to it, the smaller, quieter, Ile St-Louis. *Allow 2–3 hours.*

From St-Michel métro station cross the Pont St-Michel, then turn right along the quai du Marché Neuf.

1 Place du Parvis Notre-Dame

Across the vast square, created by Haussmann, stands the austere Gothic cathedral that Parisians refer to, with pride and affection, simply as Notre-Dame (*see pp92–3*). Gallo-Roman and medieval remains are displayed in the Crypte Archéologique, beneath the Parvis. On the south side stands the statue of Charlemagne.

The incomparable cathedral of Notre-Dame

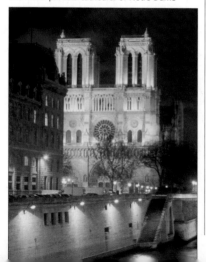

Coming out of the cathedral, turn right along the north side.

2 The Old Cloister Quarter

The rue Chanoinesse gives a fair idea of what the area looked like in the 13th century. It was here that the canons lived and taught; original houses at Nos 22 and 24 bring to mind the moving story of Héloïse and Abélard (*see p60*). *Turn left along quai de la Corse, then left again into rue de la Cité.*

3 Place Louis-Lépine

During the week, the square is the site of a colourful flower market, and on Sundays a no less picturesque but noisier bird market takes place. *Continue along rue de Lutèce. Facing are the Palais de Justice, the law courts and the Ste-Chapelle. Turn right, then left along quai de l'Horloge, past the Conciergerie, to reach place Dauphine.*

4 Place Dauphine

This is a haven of peace where you can stop at one of the small restaurants and admire two of the original 17th-century brick and stone houses at Nos 12 and 14. Beyond the statue of Henri IV, the square du Vert Galant affords beautiful views of the river.

Cross over to the Left Bank, turn left and follow the embankment, lined with bookstalls, past Notre-Dame, then cross the Pont de l'Archevêché and the Pont St-Louis and turn left.

5 Quai de Bourbon

In striking contrast to the feverish activity of the Cité and the Left Bank, the Ile St-Louis offers a peaceful village atmosphere, nowhere more apparent than along the cobbled quai de Bourbon, lined with classical mansions. At the corner of rue des Deux Ponts, Au Franc Pinot, which has a restaurant in the vaulted cellars and a wine bar on the ground floor, is a pleasant place to stop.
Continue along quai d'Anjou to No 17.

6 Hôtel de Lauzun

Built by Le Vau in 1657, the Hôtel de Lauzun, with its gilded-dolphin waterspouts, had many famous occupants, including the poet Charles Pierre Baudelaire, who wrote much of *Les Fleurs du Mal* here, and the composer Wagner. It now belongs to the City of Paris.
Further on, turn right into rue St-Louis-en-l'Ile.

7 Rue St-Louis-en-l'Ile

This is the main street of the island. The 17th-century church of St-Louis has an unusual clock outside and a richly decorated interior. A few doors away, at No 31, is the ice cream specialist, Berthillon.
Turn left into rue des Deux Ponts, then cross the bridge. Facing you is the famous but expensive restaurant, La Tour d'Argent, and on your left the strangely modern Institut du Monde Arabe (see p88). Turn right and follow the embankment back to place St-Michel.

Nearby
Monnaie de Paris, churches of St-Séverin and St-Julien-le-Pauvre, place du Châtelet and Hôtel de Ville.

The Concorde

The place de la Concorde, or la Concorde, as it is simply called, is undoubtedly the most splendid square in Paris. Its impressive size, harmonious proportions and superbly elegant setting are the striking features of this true masterpiece of town planning. Because of its strategic position at the crossroads of the main east-west and north-south flows of traffic, it gets very congested at times.

The ancient obelisk dominates La Concorde

A royal square

The square was commissioned by the aldermen of Paris as a token of their admiration for Louis XV. Ambitious plans submitted by the architect Jacques-Ange Gabriel were approved and a vast area of more than 8ha (20 acres) of drained marshland was chosen on the edge of town.

The square, which was built over a period of 20 years from 1755 to 1775, was originally surrounded by a moat and balustrade, and an equestrian statue of Louis XV by Bouchardon was placed in its centre.

Tragic beginnings

Before work was completed, tragedy struck: in 1770, a huge crowd had gathered on the square to celebrate the wedding of Marie Antoinette and the future Louis XVI, when panic caused more than 100 people to be crushed to death in the moat.

Twenty-two years later, the guillotine was set up on the square, which had been renamed place de la Révolution. In 1795, the dreaded instrument was dismantled and the square renamed place de la Concorde as a symbol of hope and peace!

Reconciliation

It was not until 1836 that the name was adopted for good. The square was partly redesigned by the architect Hittorff and the decoration completed. King Louis-Philippe decided against another statue in the centre and chose instead a neutral monument, a 3,000-year-old Egyptian obelisk.

The obelisk

The obelisk, which comes from the temple of Luxor, was a gift from the viceroy of Egypt, Muhammad Ali. This imposing pink granite monolith, 23m (75ft) high and weighing 220 tons, is 3,300 years old. It is covered with hieroglyphs that detail the life of Rameses II, and the drawings on the base depict the process of dismantling and transporting it, and erecting it on its present site. The two large fountains are modelled on those in St Peter's Square in Rome.

The views from the centre of the square are magnificent. To the west are the Champs Elysées and the Arc de Triomphe, to the east the Jardin des Tuileries, the Arc de Triomphe du Carrousel and the Louvre beyond, to the north the rue Royale, closed off by the Madeleine, and to the south the Pont de la Concorde and the Assemblée Nationale across the river.

The twin mansions

The colonnades of the two identical buildings marking the entrance to the rue Royale were modelled on that of the Louvre. The Hôtel de la Marine is on the right as you face the Madeleine, and the Hôtel Crillon is on the left. This is now a world-famous luxury hotel, but in 1778, soon after it was built, it was the venue for the signing of an important treaty between France and the newly founded United States of America.

Statues round the square

To complete the decoration, eight statues representing various French towns stand in the corners of the square. Outside the Tuileries' gates are two figures on winged horses by Coysevox, representing Fame and Mercury. To complement them, the famous *Chevaux de Marly* by Coustou were brought from Louis XIV's castle to mark the entrance to the Champs Elysées. Both the sets now displayed are replicas, as the marble originals have been taken to the Louvre.

Nearby

La Madeleine, Place Vendôme, Jardin des Tuileries, Musée de l'Orangerie, Musée d'Orsay, Petit Palais and Grand Palais.

One of the enormous fountains in la Concorde

FAUBOURG ST-GERMAIN

This elegant district, bordering the Seine between the fashionable St-Germain-des-Prés and the stately Hôtel des Invalides, had its heyday in the 18th century. Two main thoroughfares, boulevard St-Germain and boulevard Raspail, cut across it, carrying fast-moving traffic, while the side streets, taken over by ministries, embassies and official residences, are wrapped in the kind of secluded atmosphere usually found in museums. Beautifully restored mansions of all sizes (some of them still privately owned) line the streets.

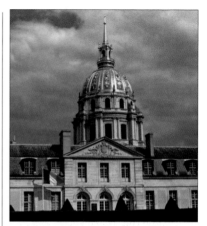
The imposing building of Les Invalides

An aristocratic district

The name *faubourg* (suburb) is the only reminder of the area's suburban beginnings, when it was open countryside surrounding the Abbey of St-Germain-des-Prés. Around 1680, the aristocracy and the rich started to move in and, in the space of 50 years, the Faubourg had supplanted the Marais as the most fashionable residential district.

Assemblée National (Palais Bourbon)

The seat of the lower house of the French Parliament (the Assemblée Nationale) consists of two 18th-century mansions: the Hôtel de Bourbon which was originally built for one of Louis XIV's illegitimate daughters, the Duchess of Bourbon, and the Hôtel de Lassay. The two were joined in 1764 and a Greek-style façade was added in the 19th century to match that of the Madeleine. On the place du Palais Bourbon, the original façade has kept its 18th-century appearance. To attend an Assemblée debate you must apply in writing.
33 bis quai d'Orsay, 75007. Tel: 01 40 63 64 08. Authorised group visits only. Métro: Assemblée Nationale.

Streets of special interest

The general plan of the district is very neat, with the main *hôtels* (private residences) having been built along five parallel streets.

Nearer the river is rue de Lille with the Hôtel de Seignelay at No 80, now the Ministère du Commerce, and the Hôtel de Beauharnais, now the German Ambassador's residence. Both were built in 1714.

Next comes rue de l'Université, so-called because the land once belonged to

Places of Interest
Musée d'Orsay (*see pp82–3*).
Musée de la Légion d'Honneur (*see p102*).
Musée Rodin (*see p91*).

the university, with some of the earliest mansions: No 78, built in 1687, and No 51, dating from 1707.

The rue St-Dominique lost a few of its 18th-century houses when the boulevard St-Germain was opened.

In rue de Grenelle, the most imposing mansion at No 110, dating from 1778, is now occupied by the Ministère de l'Education Nationale; the beautiful Fontaine des Quatre Saisons at Nos 57–9 (see p53), and the Hôtel Bouchardon next door epitomise 18th-century elegance and refinement. The Hôtel Biron (the Musée Rodin) and the Hôtel Matignon (the office and home of the prime minister), at 77 and 57 rue de Varenne respectively, are probably the two most beautiful mansions of the whole district.

Grands boulevards

These wide thoroughfares on the Right Bank, slicing through the heart of the capital between the place de l'Opéra and the place de la Bastille, make you feel the real pace of Parisian life. Having re-placed obsolete fortifications at the end of the 17th century, the boulevards became a popular place for strolling. However, a marked difference soon developed between east and west, the latter being the fashionable end. Today, it is still fascinating to notice the change as you walk east from the Opéra. Just off the boulevard des Italiens on the right is the Opéra Comique specialising in light opera. In the boulevard Montmartre on the left is the Musée Grévin, the famous waxworks, while on either side of the boulevard are two 19th-century shopping arcades.

Further east, two 17th-century monumental gates mark the entrance to the boulevard St-Denis and the boulevard St-Martin. South of the boulevard de Bonne Nouvelle is a rather seedy district called Le Sentier, a centre of the wholesale trade in fabrics and ready-made clothes.

Nearby
Les Invalides (see pp56–7).
Church of St-Germain-des-Prés (see p41).
Musée Delacroix (see p107).

The beautiful rococo Hôtel Biron, on boulevard des Invalides, houses the Musée Rodin

Fountains

Paris has many public fountains of all shapes and sizes, faithfully reflecting the architectural style of their time. Some, like the Fontaine des Quatre Saisons in the Faubourg St-Germain, were once the only means of water supply in the whole district. Others, like the Fontaine des Quatre Points Cardinaux on place St-Sulpice, were purely ornamental.

The Fontaine des Quatre Points Cardinaux

Fontaine du Châtelet
This is one of the 15 fountains that Napoleon had built in the city. Dating from 1808, it is sometimes referred to as the Fontaine de la Victoire because it commemorates the Emperor's victories in Italy and Egypt. Most often, though, it is called the Fontaine du Palmier because its column suggests a palm tree.
Place du Châtelet, 75001, near the Hôtel de Ville. Métro: Châtelet.

Fontaine Cuvier
This very ornate fountain is dedicated to Georges Cuvier, the 19th-century zoologist who founded the study of comparative anatomy. Notice the crocodile turning its head round, something crocodiles apparently cannot do!
Corner of rue Linné and rue Cuvier, 75005, near the Jardin des Plantes. Métro: Jussieu or Monge.

Fontaine des Innocents
This Renaissance fountain gets its name from the 12th-century Sts-Innocents Church demolished at the end of the 18th century. Built in 1550 at the corner of the rue St-Denis by the architect Pierre Lescot and the sculptor Jean Goujon, it was later moved to the centre of the square and restored in 1865, when the original reliefs round the base were removed to the Louvre.
Square des Innocents, 75001, near Les Halles. Métro: Les Halles or Châtelet.

Fontaine Louvois
This ornamental fountain by Visconti is a typical example of the decorative style used in urban architecture during the 19th century. The statues represent four French rivers: the Seine, Loire, Saône and Garonne.
Square Louvois, 75002, near the Bibliothèque Nationale. Métro: Bourse.

Fontaine de Médicis
This is the most romantic fountain in Paris and one of the main attractions of the Jardin du Luxembourg. Built in 1624 by Salomon de Brosse for Marie de Medici, Henri IV's widow, it is in the Italian style fashionable at the time.
Jardin du Luxembourg, 75006. Métro: Odéon. RER: Luxembourg.

Fontaine Molière

Situated at the intersection of rues de Richelieu and Molière, this fountain is dedicated to the famous 17th-century playwright who died at No 40 rue de Richelieu. Built by Visconti in 1844, it shows the writer deeply absorbed in his thoughts.

Rue de Richelieu, 75001, near the Palais-Royal.
Métro: Palais-Royal or Pyramides.

Fontaine de l'Observatoire

This bronze fountain by Davioud dates from 1873. It depicts the different parts of the world – Europe, Asia, Africa and America – but not Oceania, which would have spoilt the symmetry of the composition. It is also called Fontaine des Quatre Parties du Monde.

Avenue de l'Observatoire, 75006, south of the Luxembourg gardens.
RER: Port-Royal or Luxembourg.

Fontaine des Quatre Points Cardinaux

Standing in the centre of the charming place St-Sulpice, this fountain is the work of the architect Visconti. Facing the four cardinal points of the compass are the busts of four well-known men of the church who never became cardinals.

Place St-Sulpice, 75006.
Métro: St-Sulpice, Mabillon.

Fontaine des Quatre Saisons

The street is too narrow to get a good view of this beautiful 18th-century fountain by Bouchardon. In the centre, the city of Paris looks down on the rivers Seine and Marne, while on either side are figures representing the seasons.

57–59 rue de Grenelle, 75007, at the heart of the Faubourg St-Germain.
Métro: Rue du Bac.

Fontaine St-Michel

This monumental fountain was built by Davioud during the Second Empire and is typical of the ornate style in fashion at the time. It is the favourite meeting place for young Parisians.

Place St-Michel, 75005, in the Latin Quarter.
Métro: St-Michel.

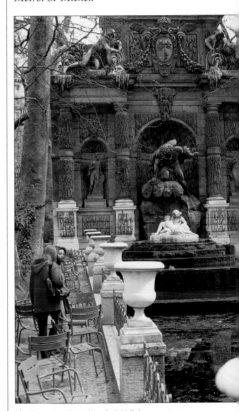

The baroque Fontaine de Médicis

LES HALLES

This is very much an up-and-coming district, developing round the ultramodern Forum des Halles and rapidly regaining the popularity it lost as a result of the departure of the colourful but obsolete food market that gave the area its name (*halles* means covered market). Combined with that of Beaubourg nearby, its renovation, undertaken during the 1970s, has proved a commercial success. (*See* Walk *pp38–9.*)

Tradition versus modernisation

There was a great deal of controversy in Paris about the destruction of the 19th-century Pavillons Baltard, which housed the old market, for which Parisians suddenly discovered a deep attachment. Firmly rooted traditions were being threatened, they felt, and would be lost forever in the pursuit of improbable benefits. However, the planners won and work went ahead.

Forum des Halles

The originality of the complex lies in the fact that there is little to be seen from the street: galleries on four levels run round a huge crater, which provides ample daylight in the central square. From there, a maze of underground

LE VENTRE DE PARIS

The 'belly of Paris' was the evocative name given to the area in the 19th century by the novelist Emile Zola. At that time, it had been the main food supply centre of the city for centuries, growing until it reached bursting point. The Pavillons Baltard, built between 1854 and 1866, gave the market a new lease of life. However, 100 years later, the market area became congested again, and the 'belly' of Paris moved out of town to Rungis, just south of the city.

A popular commercial and cultural complex, Les Halles

'streets', lined with shops, snack bars, cinemas and restaurants, and with direct access to the métro, covers an area of 7ha (83,721sq yd); large maps are available on each level to direct you to the shops of your choice (*see p39*). On level 1 is a museum: the **Nouveau Musée Grévin** (*see p86*), an annexe of the waxworks in the boulevard Montmartre, depicting Paris at the turn of the 20th century.

Hôtel de Ville

In the newest part of the complex, beyond the place Carrée on level 3, a cultural and commercial area includes an auditorium and a video library, as well as sports facilities and a glass swimming pool.

Old streets

At ground level, round the gardens, which offer a pleasant contrast to the feverish underground activity, the old streets have preserved the character of the former market district, and many of the food shops, cafés and restaurants are still there.

Nearby Montorgueil is a lively street with vegetable stalls, cheese shops, bakeries and restaurants. While few tourists make it to this area, it is a haunt of Parisians shopping for good food. *Forum des Halles, 75001. Métro: Les Halles. RER: Châtelet.*

Hôtel de Ville

Although the present building is fairly recent, the site has always played an essential role in the history of the capital. In the Middle Ages, the square in front of the town hall was called the place de Grève because it sloped down to the river (*grève* means shore). Throughout the Ancien Régime, the site was used for public executions. In 1871, during the Commune uprising, the original town hall was destroyed by fire at the same time as the Tuileries Palace was also burned down.

The present building, which is in neo-Renaissance style, dates from 1882. Its decoration is very elaborate, as was the fashion at the turn of the 20th century: numerous statues adorn the façade, and inside, at the top of a splendid staircase, there are reception rooms with beautiful crystal chandeliers and paintings. *4 place de l'Hôtel de Ville, 75004. Tel: 01 42 76 50 49. www.paris-france.org Free guided tours by appointment only (Mon–Fri). Entrance by the north door. Métro: Hôtel de Ville.*

Les Invalides

This imposing group of buildings is an outstanding example of 17th-century classical architecture, situated at the end of a vast oblong open space stretching across from the Seine. Like Versailles, it epitomises the strength and confidence of the French monarchy under Louis XIV. Moreover, the whole surrounding area, with its wide, tree-lined avenues, the Faubourg St-Germain on one side and the Champ de Mars on the other, adds to the impression of space and grandeur. Sought-after by wealthy Parisians, it has become a quiet, secluded residential district.

NAPOLEON'S TOMB

In 1861, the architect Visconti designed a dramatic setting for the Emperor's tomb. In the centre of an open crypt the red porphyry sarcophagus was placed on a base of green granite from the Vosges. Visitors can view it from the encircling balustrade.

A pensioner's home

At the beginning of his reign, Louis XIV had difficulty in establishing himself on the throne of France, and realised the importance of a strong army. However, because of the appalling conditions faced by wounded soldiers, recruitment was difficult. In order to encourage potential recruits the king decided, in 1670, to found a hospital and pension home for 4,000 invalid ex-soldiers. Work started in 1671 and lasted for five years.

A shining monument

The king then commissioned the young architect Jules Hardouin-Mansart to design a church with a magnificent gilt dome. In 1840, after years of negotiation with the British government, Napoleon's remains were returned to France and officially buried in the Eglise du Dôme, and Les Invalides became a symbol of the Emperor's glory.

The Esplanade des Invalides

The best way to approach the Invalides is from the Pont Alexandre III (*see p34*). The vast esplanade, designed by Robert de Cotte at the beginning of the 18th century, is 500m (547yd) long and 250m (273yd) wide. From here you can enjoy sweeping views of the harmonious ensemble of buildings. A formal garden, surrounded by a dry moat, has 17th- and 18th-century bronze heavy guns; beyond it, the impressive doorway,

The Dôme church with its gilded cupola

flanked by twin pavilions, is adorned with an equestrian statue of Louis XIV, dating from 1815.

The Cour d'Honneur
The paved courtyard is lined with arcades on two storeys. Four pavilions have dormer windows adorned with trophies, and in the four corners, at roof level, there are carved horses trampling the emblems of war. More heavy guns complete this imposing setting. On either side of the courtyard are the collections of the **Musée de l'Armée** (*see* Museums, *p84*), while at the end is the entrance to St-Louis church.

St-Louis-des-Invalides
This is the original church by Libéral Bruant, also known as the soldiers' church, a cold building decorated only with flags and standards taken from the enemy. The Eglise du Dôme is visible through a glass panel behind the altar. The magnificent organ was used for the premiere of Berlioz's *Requiem* in 1837. *Open: 10am–5pm, 6pm in summer.*

Eglise du Dôme
The Eglise du Dôme was built between 1677 and 1735. The tiered façade with Doric and Corinthian columns is adorned with statues of St-Louis, Charlemagne and the four virtues, and enhanced by the well-proportioned dome. The interior is magnificently decorated with different marbles, painted cupolas, columns and low reliefs. In the side chapels are the tombs of several of Napoleon's generals as well as those of Turenne, Lyautey and Foch.

Hôtel des Invalides, 75007. Eglise du Dôme and Musée de l'Armée; tel: 01 44 42 37 72. Open: 10am–5pm, until 6pm Apr, May, Sept, until 7pm in summer. Admission charge gives access to the church and five museums. Métro: Invalides or Varenne.

Nearby
Palais Bourbon, **Faubourg St-Germain** (*see p50*); **Champ de Mars** (*see p58*); **Tour Eiffel** (*see pp110–11*); **Pont Alexandre III** (*see p34*); **Musée Rodin** (*see p91*).

Les Invalides still houses some old veterans

Walk: from the Trocadéro to Les Invalides

This is the Paris of grand vistas and wide-open spaces, where various architectural styles help to create an impressive setting for the most famous of the city's monuments, the Eiffel Tower.

Allow 2 to 3 hours (excluding museum visits and a climb to the top of the Eiffel Tower).

Begin from the Trocadéro métro station.

1 Place du Trocadéro

From the top of the Chaillot hill, the rather dull place du Trocadéro offers stunning views of the Left Bank. Several wide avenues radiating from it give the impression of a busy roundabout where no one cares to stop. Behind a high wall to the west is the Passy cemetery and, facing the river, the Palais de Chaillot, built for the 1937 Exposition Universelle. The name Trocadéro commemorates the capture in 1823 of Fort Trocadéro in Spain.

Pass between the curved wings of the Palais de Chaillot.

2 Jardins du Trocadéro

Stairs lead down to the gardens on either side of a long pool adorned with stone and gilt bronze statues and attractive floodlit fountains, which provide one of the most spectacular summer night shows of the capital.

Cross the Pont d'Iéna, named to commemorate Napoleon's victory over the Prussians in 1806. The bridge provides a good close-up view of the Eiffel Tower.

3 Champ de Mars

If, after the thrill of climbing up to the third floor of the Eiffel Tower, you feel the need to relax in a down-to-earth restaurant, then La Fontaine de Mars, 129 rue St-Dominique, is just what you are looking for. The vast open space, stretching from the Eiffel Tower to the Ecole Militaire, was originally designed in the 18th century as a parade ground for the nearby military academy, hence its name. Later on, it became the tradition to use it for large-scale public festivals and World Exhibitions; in 1989, almost half a million people attended the mammoth celebrations for the 100th birthday of the Eiffel Tower.

Walk across the park and turn right into avenue de la Motte Picquet.

4 Ecole Militaire

The building of this magnificent neoclassical military academy, designed by Louis XV's architect, Jacques-Ange Gabriel, was actually financed by a special tax on playing cards. Napoleon Bonaparte was undoubtedly its most famous cadet, passing out as a lieutenant

in the artillery with the comment: 'Will go far, given favourable circumstances'. The school is still used as an instruction centre and is closed to the public.
As you walk round the building, you might enjoy a short detour to the antique shops of the Village Suisse across the avenue de Suffren.

5 UNESCO Building

Inaugurated in 1958, this building is the result of three international architects – an American, an Italian and a Frenchman – working together on the project, while the decoration was left to famous artists: Henry Moore (monumental sculpture), Alexander Calder (mobile), Pablo Picasso (mural), Joan Miró (ceramics), Lurçat and Le Corbusier (tapestries) and Isamu Noguchi (fountain).
Follow avenue de Lowendal and walk to

No 51 bis, boulevard de la Tour Maubourg.

6 Musée de L'Ordre de la Libération

The order, created by General de Gaulle in 1940, is the highest honour bestowed by France in recognition of outstanding services rendered during World War II. Among the allied leaders honoured are: King George VI, Winston Churchill and General Eisenhower.
Tel: 01 47 05 04 10. Open: 10am–5pm (until 6pm summer). Closed: first Monday of the month. Retrace your steps and turn left. Go through the Hôtel des Invalides (see pp56–7), and walk across the Esplanade to the Invalides métro station.

Nearby
Southwest: Village Suisse antique shops.
Musée Rodin (see p91).

Latin Quarter

This is one of the oldest districts of Paris, rich in traditions going back to the Middle Ages, yet teeming with new ideas launched by its lively young population. Situated on the Left Bank, opposite the Ile-de-la-Cité, the district spreads from the place St-Michel uphill to the Montagne Ste-Geneviève dominated by the Panthéon and the Sorbonne. A free and easy atmosphere pervades the whole area.

The Gallo-Roman city
Roman public buildings were concentrated on the Left Bank, just across the river from the Ile-de-la-Cité occupied by the Celts. Ruins of public baths were discovered next to the Hôtel de Cluny, and those of an amphitheatre in the vicinity of the Jardin des Plantes. At the end of the 3rd century, hordes of barbarians burned down the whole Left Bank, halting development there for a long time.

A universal language
In the 12th century, several teachers and students broke away from the

The Law Faculty building at the Sorbonne

cathedral schools of the Ile-de-la-Cité and established themselves on the Left Bank. Their action soon led to the foundation of the university of Paris in 1215. Before the end of the 13th century, there were several colleges on the Montagne Ste-Geneviève, welcoming students from the French provinces and from many other parts of Europe as well. These early European students spoke Latin, a practice that lasted until 1789.

The Sorbonne

This was the first and most successful of the many colleges that flourished in pre-revolutionary Paris. From very humble beginnings in 1253, it developed into a reputed centre of theological studies and became the seat of the powerful university. Its prestige and popularity have survived to this day. The 17th-century buildings were extensively remodelled and enlarged at the end of the 19th century. The Sorbonne church, which is open only on special occasions, dates from the beginning of the 17th century. It contains the white marble tomb of Cardinal Richelieu.
Sorbonne: for information on a free guided tour call 01 40 46 22 11.

St-Julien-le-Pauvre

There has been a church on this site since the 6th century, as it was on the route followed by pilgrims on their way to Santiago de Compostela. The present building, which dates from the late 12th century, was the university church from the 13th to the 16th century. St-Julien is now a Greek Orthodox church. Its style is transitional, partly

Architectural detail at the Sorbonne

Romanesque and partly Gothic, with a 17th-century façade.
St-Julien-le-Pauvre, rue St-Julien, 75005. Métro: St-Michel.

Hôtel de Cluny

This is one of the best examples of domestic medieval architecture. It was built in the 15th century for the abbots of the famous Cluny Abbey on the site of the ruined Roman baths. The style of the house is inspired by the Renaissance, best observed from the main courtyard. The central building has high windows and an elaborate balustrade with impressive gargoyles, while the main staircase winds up a pentagonal tower. Inside, the Musée National du Moyen Age covers all aspects of medieval art (*see p86*).
6 place Paul-Painlevé, 75005.
Tel: 01 53 73 78 16.
Open: 9.15am–5.45pm. Closed: Tue.
Admission charge.
Métro: Cluny-La Sorbonne.

Walk: the Latin Quarter

This is the centre of university life, where tiny restaurants along the side streets and cafés on the boulevard St-Michel are packed at all hours.

Allow 2 hours (excluding a visit to the Musée National du Moyen Age – Thermes de Cluny).

Start from the place St-Michel, where the impressive 1860 fountain is a favourite meeting point. Take the rue de la Huchette, rue de la Harpe and rue St-Séverin to reach the church of St-Séverin (see pp42–3).

1 St-Séverin Quarter

The narrow streets and alleyways have kept their picturesque medieval names, such as 'rue de la Parcheminerie' (Parchment Street). Unfortunately, the authenticity of the district is threatened by the increasing number of cheap Greek and North African restaurants, with a welcome exception: La Cochonaille. Le Caveau de la Huchette (rue de la Huchette) is a well-known jazz cellar.

Go round the back of St-Séverin, down the rue St-Jacques to the church of St-Julien-le-Pauvre and the square Viviani. Then follow the rue Galande and the rue Lagrange to the place Maubert.

2 Place Maubert

Maubert is probably a contraction of Maître Albert, the famous 13th-century teacher. At one time the hideout of thieves and cut-throats, the area has been renovated, regaining its Left Bank atmosphere. The tiny rue Maître-Albert leads down to the river from where you

get a beautiful view of Notre-Dame.

Rue de Bièvre brings you back to place Maubert.

3 St-Nicolas-du-Chardonnet

Situated a little way up the rue Monge, this unusual 17th-century church with a 20th-century façade is decorated inside with paintings by Camille Corot and Charles Le Brun, and elaborate funeral monuments.

Proceed along rue du Sommerard to Cluny House (see p86), walk up rue de la Sorbonne, past the university buildings, then left into rue Soufflot.

4 Place du Panthéon

Facing you is the vast domed Panthéon (*see p98*), dominating the whole Latin Quarter. You can sit at one of the cafés and admire the view before going round to the left, past the bibliothèque Ste-Geneviève, famous for its ancient manuscripts.

Pass between the Panthéon and the highly original church of St-Etienne-du-Mont (see p40) and turn right into rue Clotilde, then left into rue de l'Estrapade.

5 Place de la Contrescarpe

This tiny square has been famous since the Middle Ages for its *cabaret de la*

Pomme de Pin (at No 1), described by the famous author, François Rabelais. There is a choice of interesting cafés and restaurants here.

Following rue Lacépède to the end, you will arrive at the Fontaine Cuvier (see p52). Turn left into rue Monge.

6 Arènes de Lutèce

Rue des Arènes, on the right, leads to the ruins of a Roman theatre, discovered during the remodelling of medieval Paris in the 19th century, and now part of a public garden.

Turn left at the crossroads, right into rue Clovis, right into rue Descartes, then bear left down rue de l'Ecole Polytechnique.

7 Collège de France

Since its foundation by François I in 1530, the college has maintained a tradition of independent teaching, and gives free public lectures on a wide range of subjects.

Continue along rue des Ecoles past square Paul-Painlevé. Cross boulevard St-Michel.

8 Rue Hautefeuille

This old, picturesque street on your right, by the former Ecole de Médecine, takes you back to place St-André-des-Arts (*see* rue St-André-des-Arts, *p109*).

Nearby
Jardin du Luxembourg, Jardin des Plantes.

Louvre

Situated on the Right Bank, within a stone's throw of the Ile-de-la-Cité, the Louvre expanded according to the whim of successive French monarchs, and today it is one of the world's largest royal palaces. It is better known, however, for the great museum within its walls. The Grand Louvre project was designed to modernise and smarten it up, and the eye-catching glass pyramid erected in the open courtyard has renewed interest in the building's 'threatened' architectural beauty.

The Musée du Louvre from the Cour Napoléon

The Louvre Palace
The original castle was consistently extended westwards, away from the congested part of the city.

The Medieval Fortress
Built by King Philippe-Auguste at the end of the 12th century, the Louvre castle was just a massive keep surrounded by a wall and towers, designed as part of the city's fortifications. It became a royal residence when Charles V extended the city further west and protected it with new fortifications. Remains of this fortress were discovered under the Cour Carrée, and have been excavated recently as part of the Grand Louvre scheme (access through the museum).

The Renaissance Palace
Until the 16th century, the Louvre was neglected in favour of less austere residences in the Marais or on the Loire; then Francis I had part of the obsolete fortress razed, and in 1546 he commissioned Pierre Lescot to build a new palace. Lescot worked on it until his death in 1571, entrusting the decoration to the sculptor Jean Goujon.

The Tuileries
Catherine de Médicis, Henri II's widow, initiated the extension of the Louvre westwards. She commissioned Philibert Delorme to build a new palace close to the Louvre, known as the Tuileries. Superstition prevented the queen from settling in here – an astrologer told her she would die there. In 1871 it was burned down and had to be demolished.

The Galerie du Bord de l'Eau
Catherine de Médicis had originally intended to link the two palaces by way of a long wing, but these plans were abandoned until Henri IV's accession to the throne. He completed the link in 1608 by having the Galerie du Bord de l'Eau and the Pavillon de Flore built.

The Cour Carrée
Louis XIII and Louis XIV concentrated their efforts on the Cour Carrée. In

1624, the architect Lemercier built the Pavillon de l'Horloge in the centre of the west wing, which he extended by another building faithfully matching that of Pierre Lescot. The other three sides were completed by Louis XIV's architects: Le Vau, Le Brun and Perrault, who also rebuilt the Apollo wing linking the Cour Carrée to the Galerie du Bord de l'Eau. The impressive Colonnade marks the formal entrance to the palace.

Squatters in the Louvre
Abandoned in favour of Versailles at the end of the 17th century, the palace was neglected and taken over by artists and their families; eventually, an assortment of buildings concealed the beautiful façades which were threatened with dilapidation. However, in 1793, the Galerie du Bord de l'Eau was turned into a museum.

The Carrousel
Napoleon settled in the Tuileries and restored order to the architectural jumble; he also commissioned Percier and Fontaine to build the Arc de Triomphe du Carrousel and a north wing along the rue de Rivoli, which Napoleon III completed.

The Grand Louvre
The purpose of this project, which began in 1981, was to create more room for the museum by refurbishing the north wing, the Richelieu wing, formerly occupied by the Ministère des Finances, and to provide badly needed public facilities. The well-known American architect, I M Pei,

consequently designed a vast new underground entrance hall over which stands a glass pyramid. The project was completed in 1999.

Palais du Louvre, 75001. For opening times, see p67. Métro: Palais-Royal.

Nearby
Jardin des Tuileries, Louvre des Antiquaires, Oratoire du Louvre, Churches of St-Roch and St-Germain-l'Auxerrois, Pont des Arts, Musée d'Orsay.

The pyramid is illuminated at night

The Louvre Museum

Francis I started the royal collection in the 16th century by acquiring 12 paintings by Italian masters, which included Leonardo da Vinci's *Mona Lisa*, still the most famous of the museum's art treasures. During the reign of Louis XIV, the king's minister, Colbert, practised a policy of systematic buying, and the collection swelled to more than 2,000 paintings.

One of the many treasures in the sculpture gallery

Meanwhile, the Académie Royale de Peinture et de Sculpture, founded in 1648, was already holding its annual exhibition in the Louvre and artists were granted lodgings in the palace. Shortly after the creation of the museum in 1793, works of art were brought back from Versailles, and later Napoleon and his successors continued to enrich the collections with Greek, Assyrian and Egyptian antiquities.

The Carrousel du Louvre

In order to avoid unnecessary delays, use the direct access from the Palais-Royal métro station to the museum through the new Carrousel du Louvre, a vast underground architectural complex that forms part of the Grand Louvre project and links the Jardin des Tuileries to the Louvre. It includes the Galerie du Carrousel, a wide alleyway lit at one end by an inverted glass pyramid and leading to the museum's entrance hall.

The museum today

The Louvre consists of three wings, Sully, Denon and Richelieu, which house the museum's seven departments identifiable by a colour code. The collections are displayed on four levels, each divided into 10 *arrondissements* accessible by means of escalators from the underground reception area, where leaflets in English, including ground plans, are available to help you decide what you want to see. There are also maps and signposts throughout the museum. If you are looking for a particular work, ask a member of staff to direct you in case there has been a rearrangement of exhibits.

The medieval moat

The Sully escalator leads directly to rooms depicting the history of the palace and surrounding area; from there you can go to the Sully region, or walk round the moat of the medieval fortress buried under the Cour Carrée. Objects found during the excavations include Charles VI's gilt helmet (14th-century).

Oriental antiquities

This department houses archaeological finds from the valleys of the Euphrates and the Tigris, concerning mainly the Sumerian and Babylonian civilisations, the Elamite and Persian civilisations, the Phoenicians and the Assyrians.

Egyptian antiquities

The great Sphinx in pink granite makes a most impressive introduction to Egyptian art, while the Seated Scribe, dating from around 2500 BC, and the bust of Amenophis IV from Karnak are strikingly realistic masterpieces.

Greek, Etruscan and Roman antiquities

You cannot visit the Louvre Museum without seeing the 2nd century BC sculpture of *Venus de Milo*, generally acknowledged as a perfect example of feminine beauty.

Paintings

Several paintings by Leonardo da Vinci, Titian and Raphael are among the most outstanding works of the Italian school. Flemish and Dutch painters include Rembrandt and Van Dyck. There is also a superbly dramatic *Christ en croix* by El Greco. The French school is strongly represented by de la Tour, Poussin, Watteau, Delacroix and Géricault.

Sculpture

Of special interest are *Les Nymphes* by Jean Goujon, *Les Chevaux de Marly* by Guillaume Coustou, a copy of which guards the entrance to the Champs Elysées, several busts by Houdon, and the *Esclaves* by Michelangelo.

Objets d'art

The Crown Jewels, including the Regent, a 140-carat diamond, are the biggest attractions here. Among a wealth of other fine pieces are the Maximilian tapestries and furniture by Boulle.

Musée du Louvre, Palais du Louvre, 75001, Paris Cedex 01. Tel: 01 40 20 51 51. www.louvre.fr. Open: 9am–6pm; Wed & Fri to 9.45pm. Closed: Tue. Admission charge. Facilities: bookshop, audio guides, auditorium, restaurant and cafeteria which stay open after closing time. Main entrance under the glass pyramid in the Cour Napoléon. Métro: Palais-Royal.

The Louvre's vast collection of art includes many acknowledged masterpieces

Today, foreigners account for one-sixth of the capital's population; thus, over the last few decades, the character of certain areas has drastically changed. Some minorities, such as the White Russians, are fully assimilated, even if they still get together on occasions. Others, however, live in enclaves that, over the years, have acquired a strong cultural identity.

The Jewish district is situated at the heart of the Marais, within a small quadrangle formed by rue de Rivoli, rue des Francs Bourgeois, rue Vieille-du-Temple and rue de Sévigné. There has been a Jewish community in this area since the Middle Ages, but the arrival in 1962 of a great number of Algerian Jews suddenly altered the east European flavour of the district. The rue des Rosiers is very picturesque, with its delicatessens, restaurants, felafel snack bars and old food shops turned into fashion boutiques.

During the 1960s, tower-block flats mushroomed in the 13th *arrondissement* and, as a result, a large number of Asian immigrants, the majority of them Chinese, settled in the area surrounding the porte de Choisy. As a result, the avenue d'Ivry is particularly lively with its cinemas, restaurants, supermarkets, and shops that look like pagodas.

Successive waves of immigrants, this time mainly from Africa, have settled in the Goutte-d'Or district, just east of Montmartre, and now, more than 30 different nationalities cohabit in what must truthfully be called deteriorating conditions. Redevelopment is in the air, under-standably opposed by the locals, for what will become of the colourful little shops that do a roaring trade selling exotic groceries, junk jewellery and African fabrics?

Colonial connections, refugees and other immigrant groups are evident in the vibrant, cosmopolitan atmosphere of Paris's ethnic commercial ventures

The Marais

This is one of the most authentic districts of Paris, with a wealth of 17th-century domestic architecture. It is also a lively area, where traditions are being rediscovered, and where variety and contrasts make strolling along its picturesque streets a real pleasure.

A new lease of life for the mansions in the Marais

Against all odds
Only 30 years ago the Marais seemed to have irretrievably sunk back into its murky beginnings. The name means marshy land, and this is exactly what it was until, in the 13th century, various religious communities, including the Knights Templars, turned it into arable land. At the beginning of the 17th century, Henri IV had the place Royale (now the place des Vosges) built right at the heart of the district, and the aristocracy promptly commissioned the most renowned architects to design the splendid mansions (*hôtels*) seen there today. This was the Marais' golden age. But then fashion changed and the district, deserted by the wealthy in favour of the Faubourg St-Germain, was taken over by shopkeepers and craftsmen, while the beautiful mansions gradually became dilapidated.

A new lease of life
In the early 1960s, the Ministre de la Culture, André Malraux, made the district a protected area and restoration work began immediately. The Marais assumed its cultural heritage while offering its inhabitants a new quality of life. Some *hôtels* were cleverly converted into flats or turned into museums, and new shopkeepers moved in and set up smart boutiques. An artistic revival followed, which is still very apparent.

Interesting streets
It is certainly worth taking your time, and even losing your way in the side streets north of the rue des Francs Bourgeois. There are also lively streets, which you don't want to miss. Stretching from one end of the Marais to the other, the rue des Francs Bourgeois is a commercial street lined with many fine houses, boutiques, cafés and restaurants. The rue des Archives is well known for its leather goods and jewellery. The rue Vieille-du-Temple has an assortment of restaurants, cafés and quaint shops, and the rue des Rosiers is the picturesque main street of the Jewish Quarter. South of the wide rue St-Antoine, the area of rue St-Paul and the Village St-Paul is a must for antiques lovers.

Some beautiful mansions
The Hôtel Carnavalet in the rue de Sévigné is a Renaissance mansion remodelled by Mansart in the 17th century. Madame de Sévigné lived in it for 20 years and wrote many of her famous letters there. It now houses the Musée de l'Histoire de Paris.

Across rue des Francs Bourgeois is the 1584 Hôtel de Lamoignon, one of the oldest mansions in the district.

At the corner of rue des Archives and rue des Francs Bourgeois, the **Hôtel de Soubise** is an early 18th-century residence, but its corbelled turrets are a reminder of the original 14th-century manor house. Since 1808 it has been the home of the National Archives.

The Hôtel de Sens, in rue du Figuier, is one of the few remaining medieval residences – it was built in the late-15th century. Notice the turrets and the beautiful courtyards. In rue des Archives, the Hôtel Guénégaud, built in 1650, houses the **Musée de la Chasse et de la Nature**, which has a collection of arms as well as pictures by Vernet, Oudry and Chardin, and tapestries based on the theme of hunting.

St-Paul-St-Louis

This baroque church, which was completed in 1641, was modelled on the Gesù church in Rome. The interior is well lit and richly decorated; in the transept there is a *Christ au Jardin des Oliviers* by Delacroix.

Nearby
Hôtel de Sully 62 rue St-Antoine.
Place des Vosges (see p98).

Museums
Musée Cognacq Jay Hotel Donon
(see p86); **Musée de l'Histoire de France**, Hôtel de Soubise, 60 rue des Francs Bourgeois (see p87); **Musée Picasso** Hôtel Salé (see p90); **Musée de la Chasse et de la Nature** 60 rue des Archives. Tel: 01 53 01 92 40. Open: 11am–5.15pm (later in summer). Admission charge. Métro: Hôtel de Ville.

Rest your feet, enjoy a drink and watch the world go by at a Marais café

Walk: the Marais

This area of great architectural wealth is a fashionable residential district enlivened by a variety of small shops and restaurants, art galleries and craft workshops.

Allow 2 hours (excluding museum visits).

Begin from the place St-Gervais (métro Hôtel de Ville). Facing is St-Gervais-St-Protais, the oldest classical church in Paris.

1 Rue François-Miron

One of the first roads to cross the marshy area or *marais*, the street is lined with old houses of interest: Nos 11 and 13 are half-timbered, 15th-century houses; Nos 44 to 46 have splendid Gothic cellars; and further up, the 17th-century Hôtel de Beauvais (No 68) rang with Mozart's music when the young prodigy stayed there in 1763. The baroque church of St-Paul-St-Louis stands at the beginning of rue St-Antoine.

2 Rue St-Antoine

This has been the main street of the Marais since the 14th century, when it was a favourite venue for jousting contests. Henri II was fatally wounded here in 1559 in a tournament to celebrate his daughter's wedding.

The rue de Sévigné opposite the church leads to place du Marché-Ste-Catherine where you will find a good selection of restaurants. The courtyard of the 1625 Hôtel de Sully (No 62) has impressive sculptures featuring the seasons and the elements.
Turn left into rue de Birague, leading to the place des Vosges (see pp98–9). Take rue des Francs Bourgeois going west, then turn right into rue de Sévigné.

3 Rues du Parc Royal and Payenne

On your left is the imposing Hôtel Carnavalet which houses the Musée Historique de la Ville de Paris. Turn left at the end of the street; a row of lovely mansions facing a peaceful garden make a perfect setting. In rue Payenne, opposite two elegant mansions, is another garden adorned with statues.
Turn right.

4 Rue des Francs Bourgeois

Its medieval name, referring to the almshouses built in the 14th century for the non tax-paying citizens or *francs bourgeois*, and the house of Jean Hérouët (No 54), with its elegant turret, both recall the days when the street was the

centre of the weaving trade. Today it is lined with 17th- and 18th-century mansions, boutiques, and restaurants such as L'Orée du Marais at No 29.
Turn right into rue Vieille-du-Temple, then right into rue de la Perle.

5 Musée de la Serrure

Housed in a smaller-scale mansion, once the home of the architect who built Les Invalides, the museum's collection traces the history of locks since Roman times.
Open: Mon–Fri 10am–noon, 2–5pm. Closed: weekends.

Rue de Thorigny opposite leads to the Musée Picasso (see p90). Turn back down rue de la Perle and walk along rue des 4 Fils; on the right is the Musée de la Chasse et de la Nature (see p71); turn left into rue des Archives, then left again into rue des Francs Bourgeois, past the Hôtel de Soubise.

6 Notre-Dame-des-Blancs-Manteaux

This church is famous for its woodwork, in particular its rococo pulpit and organ loft. Concerts are given here during the Marais festival.
Return to the rue des Archives. Turn left.

7 Cloître des Billettes

Built in the 15th century as part of a monastery, this is the only medieval cloister left in Paris. The church next door is 18th-century.

Nearby
Centre Pompidou, Hôtel de Sens, Village-St-Paul, The Bastille.

Montmartre

The distinctive white outline of the Sacré-Coeur basilica, visible from almost anywhere in the city, is the universally recognised symbol of Montmartre. The name Montmartre draws on people's imaginations to keep alive the memory of its heyday. For, unlike other districts, La Butte relies entirely on its past image for survival. Quite often it looks like a vast open-air theatre where the décor never changes and the same play is enacted every day.

TOULOUSE-LAUTREC

Born into the aristocracy and crippled at an early age, Toulouse-Lautrec led a sad life made endurable by his talent and passion for painting. He portrayed scenes of Montmartre's nightlife, sketching its stars with unique realism.

Artwork lines the streets

The case of Montmartre is unique, for it was its picturesque rural atmosphere and its free and 'easy' life that caught the world's attention at a time when most cities were overwhelmed with industrial squalor. It had nothing to offer except its refreshing simplicity, and its artists. The artists are back and a few cafés and cabarets full of memories remain, but the heritage is very difficult to preserve in a rapidly changing city with a growing tourist trade.

The most interesting parts of Montmartre are today centred round rue Lepic and its market, as well as the place des Abbesses and the surrounding area. However, it is worth strolling along rue des Saules or in the place du Tertre: do it early in the morning or out of season if you want to avoid the crowds.

Bohemian life

It all began in the early 19th century, when a few artists and writers wishing to lead a freer life settled on the Butte: Berlioz, Nerval and Heine were three of the earliest residents. After the Franco-Prussian war of 1870, Montmartre became the centre of Paris's bohemian life, inhabited by impoverished painters and poets, and visited by Parisians who flocked into the cabarets, cafés and dance halls.

At the turn of the 20th century, the most famous of these establishments were the Chat Noir and the Moulin Rouge at the foot of the hill, the Moulin de la Galette halfway up in rue Lepic, La Bonne Franquette at the corner of rue des Saules and rue St-Rustique, and the Lapin Agile down on the other side of the hill. Artists like Renoir, Van Gogh and Toulouse-Lautrec found their inspiration among the enthusiastic spectators and the colourful performers. They were succeeded by Utrillo, Picasso, Braque, Modigliani and many others. This lasted until World War I, when the artists left for Montparnasse.

Musée de Montmartre

Number 12 rue Cortot is one of the oldest houses on the Butte, dating from the 17th century. The museum depicts the history of Montmartre through mementoes of its most famous inhabitants.
Métro: Abbesses.

St-Pierre-de-Montmartre

This is one of the oldest churches in Paris, once part of the powerful Abbey of Montmartre. Built in the 12th century, it has an 18th-century façade. Inside there are some fine carvings on the Romanesque capitals, contrasting with the modern stained glass, as well as four marble columns, probably belonging to a Roman temple that stood on the site.

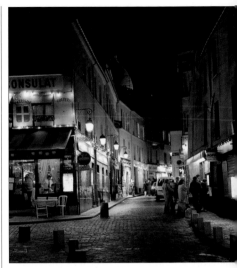
Montmartre, still a village at heart

Cimetière de Montmartre

Access to the cemetery is by a flight of stairs on the left of rue Caulaincourt, at the end of the bridge as you walk towards the boulevard de Clichy. Ask for a map at the entrance. Many famous artists and writers are buried here, among them the novelists Stendhal and Zola, the composer Berlioz, the poets Heine and Vigny, the painter Degas and, more recently, the film director François Truffaut.
Rue Caulaincourt. Métro: Abbesses or Lamarck-Caulaincourt.

> **Nearby**
> **Sacré-Coeur** (see p100).
> **Musée de Montmartre** *12 rue Cortot. Tel: 01 46 06 61 11. Open: 11am–6pm. Closed: Mon. Admission charge.*
> **Espace Dali** *11 rue Poulbot. Tel: 01 42 64 40 10. Open: 10am–6pm. Admission charge.*

Walk: Montmartre

Although it remains a symbol of bohemian life, La Butte has lost some of its romantic appeal. Sometimes, however, a walk along the quaint old streets can take you back a hundred years. This is the area featured in the popular 2001 film, *Le fabuleux destin d'Amélie Poulain.*
Allow 2 hours.

Begin from the Pigalle métro station.

1 Pigalle

For 100 years the name has been associated with a kind of exuberant and colourful nightlife, usually summed up in two words: Moulin Rouge. That famous institution is still as popular as ever, but the area has now been taken over by less picturesque clubs, discos, sex shops and pornographic cinemas. It is not advisable for women to walk round Pigalle at night on their own.
Walk along boulevard de Rochechouart, and turn left into rue de Steinkerque.

2 Place des Abbesses

At the end of the street, a funicular leads directly to the Sacré-Coeur Basilica. Turn left into rue Tardieu and continue along the rue Yvonne-Le-Tac: a chapel stands on the site where it is thought Saint-Denis was martyred in the 3rd century.

Notice the métro entrance on the place des Abbesses, with its glass-roofed, wrought-iron structure, originally designed by Hector Guimard at the turn of the 20th century. St-Jean l'Evangéliste, dating from the same period, was the first church to be built of concrete.
Leave by rue des Abbesses and turn right into the twisting rue Ravignan.

3 Place Emile-Goudeau
On this charming square is a reconstruction of the Bateau-Lavoir, burnt down in 1970, where Picasso and friends such as Braque, Modigliani, Juan Gris and others made history (*see p78*).
Continue to the end of rue Ravignan. Follow rue Norvins.

4 Place du Tertre
Now focused on the tourist trade, this old village square has lost its authenticity, but you can imagine what it was like in the 1920s. The tiny place du Calvaire in the southwest corner offers exceptional views of the capital.
Leave place du Tertre past the old church of St-Pierre (see p75) and walk to the Sacré-Coeur Basilica.

5 Sacré-Coeur
If you don't mind crowds, you will enjoy the majesty of the place and the vast panorama in front (*see p100*).
Walk across rue du Mont-Cenis and along rue Cortot where No 12 houses the Musée de Montmartre (see p75). Turn right at the end of the street.

6 Rue des Saules
This is one of the most picturesque streets, running downhill from the Butte. On the right is the Montmartre vineyard and, on the other side of rue St-Vincent, the Lapin Agile, hardly changed since the days of Picasso and Vlaminck. In the Cimetière St-Vincent opposite, you can see Utrillo's grave.
Walk along rue St-Vincent and turn left up some stairs to the Château des Brouillards, an 18th-century folly. Beyond is avenue Junot; turn left, then right into rue Lepic.

7 Moulin de la Galette
The old mill on your right was once a famous dance hall painted by Renoir and Van Gogh, who lived with his brother at No 54.
Follow the street to the bottom of the hill. On the corner stands the Moulin Rouge.

Sacré-Coeur, atop Paris's highest point

Ever since the 12th century, when students and tutors rejected the stifling teaching of the church and moved to the Left Bank, Paris has been a centre of attraction for artists from all over the world, and the melting pot of new art movements. This long-standing tradition reached its climax during the second half of the 19th century.

It was after 1870 that Paris really became the world's artistic centre, being both a sanctuary for misunderstood artists, such as Oscar Wilde, and the birthplace of major art movements, such as Impressionism.

The 'Bateau-Lavoir' was the romantic name of a shabby wooden building in Montmartre, which at the turn of the 20th century housed poor artists including Modigliani, Van Dongen, Juan Gris and, above all, Picasso and Braque, who developed the Cubist style as a reaction against Impressionism. Picasso's Les Demoiselles d'Avignon was painted

here. The artistic life is depicted in Puccini's opera La Bohème.

It was at that time too that Diaghilev created his Ballet Russe and that the premiere of Stravinsky's Sacre du Printemps caused a scandal at the Théâtre des Champs Elysées. The indecisive period between 1918 and 1939 was marked by the 'lost generation', a group of American writers including Gertrude Stein, Ezra Pound and Ernest Hemingway, while the Exposition Internationale des Arts Décoratifs et Industriels in 1925 launched a new style, Art Deco.

After the difficult post-World War II period, Paris is now reclaiming its position as a leader in contemporary art. This revival was sparked off by the inauguration of the Centre Pompidou, followed by other major projects such as the Opéra Bastille and La Villette, which offer a new range of artistic experiences.

Paris remains, reassuringly, a city of street artists who can provide unique mementoes of your visit – perhaps you'll spot a budding Braque or Toulouse-Lautrec

Montparnasse

Unlike Montmartre, this 'other' artists' stronghold was brutally drawn into the 20th century when a major town-planning project remodelled its centre during the 1960s and 1970s.

Paris from the Tour
Montparnasse

Olympian heights

The area was jokingly given the pompous name of Mont Parnasse (Mount Parnassus) in the 17th century by students from the Latin Quarter. In the 18th century it was a place of popular entertainment as bars, restaurants and cabarets, just outside the city boundaries, could serve tax-free wine. The tradition survived even after the district became part of Paris during the second half of the 19th century.

La 'Ruche'

Just before World War I, artists and poets suddenly moved from Montmartre to this unknown Left Bank district which soon came into the limelight, attracting painters and also composers such as Stravinsky and Satie, and later, the 'lost generation' of American writers. The wine pavilion from the 1900 Exposition Universelle was transferred to the passage de Dantzig by a patron of the arts for the benefit of needy artists; it was given the romantic name of la Ruche (the beehive), and soon welcomed Modigliani, Zadkine, Chagall and Léger. Matisse, Picasso, Braque, Klee, Miró, Ernst, Cocteau and Apollinaire all lived in Montparnasse at one time, their social life revolving round four cafés in

the boulevard Montparnasse: La Coupole, Le Select, La Rotonde and Le Dôme. Here they met with Russian political refugees like Lenin and Trotsky.

The old district

This is still centred round the Carrefour Vavin, now the place Pablo-Picasso, where the well-known café-restaurants have survived and keep the legend alive, crowded with today's intellectuals and artists. But whereas the décor has been carefully preserved, the establishments are certainly more upmarket now than in the days of Chagall. Just west of the Cimetière Montparnasse, rue de la Gaîté is, as its name implies, the centre of the district's nightlife. It is lined with cabarets, dance halls, and theatres such as the Théâtre de la Gaîté-Montparnasse and the Théâtre Montparnasse.

Cimetière de Montparnasse

The main entrance is in the boulevard Edgar-Quinet. Many writers, artists and composers are buried here: among them the poet Baudelaire, the novelist Maupassant, the critic Sainte-Beuve, the philosopher Sartre and his lifelong companion Simone de Beauvoir, the composers César Franck and Saint-Saëns, and the sculptors Rude, Bourdelle and Zadkine. On the eastern edge of the cemetery *The Kiss* is an interesting sculpture by the Romanian artist, Constantin Brancusi, who lived in Paris for many years.

Tour Montparnasse

At the heart of the new development stands the 200m (656ft) high, 59-storey Tour Montparnasse. When it was built in the early 1970s, it was Europe's tallest office block, and aroused fierce controversy. The fastest of the 25 lifts climbs 6m (20ft) per second, reaching the top floor in 39 seconds. For most Parisians, its only redeeming feature is the splendid panorama from the 56th and 59th floors. Across the pink-granite square in front of the tower is the new Gare Montparnasse.

33 avenue du Maine, 75015. Tel: 01 45 38 52 56. Open: 9.30am–11.30pm (10.30pm in winter); weekends till 11pm. Admission charge.

Musée Bourdelle

The museum occupies the house and studio of Antoine Bourdelle, a disciple of Rodin, whose bust is among the exhibits. There are also some very interesting portraits of Beethoven.

16 rue Antoine-Bourdelle. Tel: 01 49 54 73 73. Open: 10am–6pm. Closed: Mon. Admission charge. Métro: Montparnasse.

Musée de la Poste

The museum depicts the history of postal services, and has some fascinating exhibits such as the balloon used during the siege of Paris in 1870. There is also a collection of French stamps and a display of contemporary machines and methods.

34 boulevard de Vaugirard, 75015. Tel: 01 42 79 24 24. Open: 10am–6pm. Closed: Sun. Admission charge. Métros: Montparnasse (exit place Bienvenue), Pasteúr & Falguiére.

Musée Zadkine

The works of the Russian-born sculptor, Zadkine, are exhibited in the house where he lived for 40 years until his death in 1967. The majority of his works reveal his anxious nature. The various studies he made of Van Gogh are of particular interest.

100 bis rue d'Assas. Tel: 01 55 42 77 00. Open: 10am–5.30pm. Closed: Mon. Admission charge. RER: Port Royal.

Rue de la Gaîté: old theatres survive despite the street's changing character

Musée d'Orsay

Ideally situated on the Left Bank, opposite the Jardins des Tuileries, the Musée d'Orsay has taken its rightful place among the top European art museums. It is an unusual museum, housed in a converted railway station, and this allowed the curators to depart from traditional display and to avoid monotony.

The Musée d'Orsay houses a superb art collection

Gare d'Orsay

Inaugurated in 1900, the station was built on the site of the Palais d'Orsay which was burnt to the ground during the Commune of 1871. The architect, Victor Laloux, was entrusted with the delicate task of designing a station that would not deface the surrounding area, in particular the Louvre and Jardin des Tuileries just across the Seine. He concealed the glass-roofed iron structure behind a beautiful stone façade, and adorned it inside with an elaborately decorated, coffered ceiling. However, less than 40 years later it had become obsolete, its platforms being too short for new electric trains.

A museum of 19th-century art

In 1977 it was decided to convert the station into an art museum that would re-group various collections covering the period from 1848 to 1914, including the famous Impressionist collection from the Jeu de Paume.

Thus, the new museum would make the link between the Louvre and the Musée National d'Art Moderne of the Pompidou Centre. It is an absolute must for anyone interested in 19th-century art.

The museum

When the museum opened in 1986 after a number of setbacks, it was universally acclaimed for the originality of its excellent interior design.

The collections are exhibited in chronological order, on three main levels: the ground floor, the upper floor and the middle floor (in that order). In addition to the permanent collections, there are temporary exhibitions. Ground plans and leaflets in English are available near the entrance.

The **ground floor** is devoted to the period from 1848 to 1880. The sculpture section, in the central gallery, illustrates an interesting progression from the classical style of Pradier (*Sapho*) to the Romantic approach of Carpeaux, who carved the beautiful figures of the Fontaine de l'Observatoire (*see p53*). The rooms on the right and left of the gallery form the painting section; on the right, the classical trend is represented by Ingres (*La Source*), and the Romantic trend by Delacroix (*Chasse aux Lions*). Further on, there are some fine Puvis de Chavannes and early Degas. The rooms on the left show the progression from realism, with Daumier, Millet (*Les Glaneuses*), Courbet (*L'Atelier*), and the

Barbizon school headed by Corot, towards Impressionism, represented by works painted before 1870: among them the famous *Déjeuner sur l'Herbe* by Manet, *La Pie* and *Femmes au Jardin* by Monet. In the architecture section, there is an interesting model of the Opéra Garnier and its district.

The **upper floor** is entirely devoted to Impressionism from 1872 and Post-Impressionism in a splendid festival of light and colour, with works by Monet, Renoir, Sisley and Degas. Van Gogh, too, influenced by the movement, has his rightful place here; so does Cézanne, who stands apart as a pioneer of 20th-century painting.

Post-Impressionism is represented by Seurat, Toulouse-Lautrec, Henri Rousseau and his own naïve style, Gauguin and the school of Pont-Aven, Bonnard, Vuillard, and so on.

The **middle floor** painting section is devoted to Naturalism and Symbolism, which became officially recognised themes at a time when Impressionism was rejected, and to the early 20th century with artists such as Matisse and Bonnard.

The sculpture gallery presents works by Rodin and his successors. The Art Nouveau section is well headed by Gallé, Lalique and Guimard.

1 rue le Légion d'Honneur, 75007. Tel: 01 40 49 48 14. www.musee-orsay.fr. Open: Tue–Sun 9.30am–6pm (until 9.45pm on Thur). Closed: Mon. Admission charge. Facilities include: ground floor – bookshop, post office, bureau de change; upper level – coffee shop; intermediate level – restaurant. Métro: Solférino.

A truly innovative restoration and renovation effort has given a new lease of life to the old Gare d'Orsay

Museums

The Museum and Monuments Pass enables you to visit some 60 buildings in the Paris region. It is on sale at main métro stations, in participating museums, at monuments, and at the Paris Convention and Visitors Bureau, which has welcome centres around the city. National museums are free the first Sunday of every month.

Cité des Sciences et de l'Industrie
See p116.

Maison de Balzac
See p115.

Musée de l'Armée
This is one of the most comprehensive military museums in the world, with the collections housed in buildings around the main courtyard of Les Invalides (*see p57*).

The Musée de l'Armée

Galerie de l'Occident (west side)
Among the exhibits in the ground-floor rooms is, remarkably, Henri II's suit of armour. The first floor is devoted to World War I and World War II.

Galerie de l'Orient (east side)
The ground floor has frescoes of Louis XIV's campaign in Flanders in 1672, and the famous paintings by Ingres of Napoleon's coronation. On the first floor there are mementoes of Napoleon. The second floor explores the Second Empire and the Franco-Prussian war of 1870. A recently opened wing is devoted to General de Gaulle and World War II. *Hôtel des Invalides, 129 rue de Grenelle, 75007. Tel: 01 44 42 37 72. www.invalides.org. Open: daily 10am–5pm (6pm in summer). Admission charge. Métro: Tour-Maubourg.*

MODERN ART TRENDS

Fauvism: an early 20th-century trend characterised by a simplification of form and use of bright colours.

Cubism: an early 20th-century movement concerned with rendering form and volume through geometric shapes.

Abstract Art: a movement started in 1910 by Kandinsky and rejecting figurative representation of reality. Developed mainly from 1950 onwards, especially in the US with Abstract Expressionism.

Surrealism: a 1920s trend that rejected all conventions and aimed at expressing the subconscious mind.

Realism and New Realism: from 1960 onwards, they mark a return to figurative painting with the introduction of objects from everyday life.

Display in the Musée des Arts d'Afrique et d'Océanie

Musée d'Art Moderne de la Ville de Paris

The museum is housed in the Palais de Tokyo. *La Fée Electricité*, painted by Dufy for the 1937 world exhibition in Paris, is exhibited in the museum, alongside other works of 20th- and 21st-century art. (*See also p95.*)
Palais de Tokyo, 11 avenue du Président-Wilson, 75016. Tel: 01 53 67 40 00. www.mam.paris.fr. Open: 10am–6pm. Closed: Mon. Métro: Alma-Marceau.

Musée de Quai Branly

The new Musée du Quai Branly, devoted to the arts and populations of Africa, Asia, Oceania and the Americas, opened in 2006. *Tel: 01 56 61 70 00. www.quaibranly.fr. Open: Tue–Sun 10am–6.30pm (Thur 9.30pm). Closed: Mon.*

Guimet Musée des Arts Asiatiques

Founded in the 19th century by Emile Guimet, the recently renovated museum houses a major collection of Far Eastern art. Exhibits are from Cambodia, Vietnam, Burma, Nepal, Tibet and China. On the second floor there are some beautiful Chinese ceramics.
6 place d'Iéna, 75016. Tel: 01 56 52 53 00. www.museeguimet.fr. Open: 10am–6pm. Closed: Tue. Admission charge. Métro: Iéna.

Musée des Arts Décoratifs

The collections are presented chronologically in the north wing of the Louvre. The 20th-century section includes a splendid reconstruction of Jeanne Lanvin's flat, some Dubuffet paintings and sculptures, and glass objects by Gallé and Lalique. There is also a large toy collection.
107 rue de Rivoli, 75001. Tel: 01 44 55 57 50. Open: 11am–6pm; Sat & Sun 10am–6pm. Closed: Mon. Admission charge. Métro: Palais-Royal or Tuileries.

Musée de la Mode et du Textile

Housed in the Palais du Louvre, the museum charts the history of fashion and costume from the Middle Ages to the present day.
107 rue de Rivoli, 75001. Tel: 01 44 55 57 50. www.ucad.fr. Open: 11am–6pm; Sat & Sun 10am–6pm. Closed: Mon. Admission charge. Métro: Palais-Royal or Musée du Louvre.

Musée Bourdelle (*see p81*).
Musée Cernuschi (*see p113*).
Musée de la Chasse et de la Nature (*see p71*).

Musée National du Moyen Age – Thermes de Cluny

Housed in one of the few domestic medieval buildings left in Paris, on the site of ancient Roman baths (*see p61*), this is an exceptionally fine museum entirely devoted to the Middle Ages.

On the ground floor there are 15th- and 16th-century tapestries made in Holland in the *mille fleurs* style. Particularly worthy of note is a set called *La Vie Seigneuriale*, depicting the life of the aristocracy in the 16th century.

In room VIII, there are some fragments of sculpture, including 21 heads from the Galerie des Rois that were originally on the west front of Notre-Dame. Next door is the well-preserved *frigidarium* with a fine example of Roman vaulting.

On the first floor is the museum's major exhibit: a set of six tapestries from the late 15th century, called *La Dame à la Licorne* (the Lady and the Unicorn). The lovely Gothic chapel contains another set of tapestries illustrating the life of St Stephen.
6 place Paul-Painlevé, 75005. Tel: 01 53 73 78 16. www.musee-moyenage.fr. Open: 9.15am–5.45pm. Closed: Tue. Admission charge.
Métro: Cluny-La Sorbonne, St-Michel or Odéon.

Musée Cognacq-Jay

This collection of 18th-century art has found a proper setting in the recently renovated Hôtel Donon in the Marais. Paintings and pastels by Boucher, Fragonard, La Tour, Greuze, Tiepolo and Reynolds, and drawings by Watteau are enhanced by fine pieces of furniture and other objects of the same period.
8 rue Elzévir, 75003. Tel: 01 40 27 07 21. Open: 10am–5.45pm. Closed: Mon. Admission charge. Métro: St-Paul.

Musée Delacroix
See p107.

Musée Grévin

This waxworks, founded in 1882, provides good entertainment for the whole family. There are vivid historical scenes, and numerous life-size wax figures of famous people, as well as distorting mirrors.
10 boulevard Montmartre, 75009. Tel: 01 47 70 85 05. www.grevin.com. Open: Mon–Fri 10am–6.30pm, Sat–Sun 10am–7pm. Admission charge. Métro: Grands Boulevards.

Musée Gustave Moreau
See p114.

Musée Carnavalet et l'Histoire de Paris

Housed in the imposing Hôtel Carnavalet, the museum was recently extended to the Hôtel Le-Peletier-de-St-Fargeau, and covers the history of Paris from its origins to the present day. The Hôtel Carnavalet section of the museum is reached through the monumental doorway and across the courtyard with its equestrian statue of Louis XIV by Coysevox. There are some interesting scenes from 16th-century Paris life, supported by a host of details such as shop and inn signs. Upstairs are reconstructed rooms from the reigns of Louis XIV, XV and XVI, and Madame de Sévigné's apartments.

The Hôtel Le-Peletier-de-St-Fargeau is linked to the Hôtel Carnavalet, and covers the period from the French Revolution; start on the second floor. There are models of the Bastille and the guillotine, and everyday life objects, as well as a reconstruction of the Temple prison where Louis XVI was held. The ground floor deals with the first half of the 19th century through portraits of people in the limelight. The first floor follows on with the Second Empire and the great architectural schemes that were carried out during that period. The lifestyle of the early 20th century is presented through reconstructions of rooms such as Marcel Proust's bedroom. *23 rue de Sévigné, 75003. Tel: 01 44 59 58 58. www.carnavalet.paris.fr. Open: 10am–5.40pm. Closed: Mon. Admission charge. Métro: St-Paul.*

Musée de L'Histoire de France

This museum, housed in the beautiful Hôtel de Soubise, depicts French history through documents from the national archives. Of particular interest are the Edit de Nantes of 1598 recognising religious freedom, and its Révocation in 1685, which led to the exile of the Huguenots; the 1789 Déclaration des Droits de l'Homme (Declaration of Human Rights); Louis XVI's diary and Napoleon's will. Princesse de Soubise's apartments have the most exquisite rococo decorations, with paintings by Natoire, Boucher and Van Loo.
60 rue des Francs Bourgeois, 75003. Tel: 01 40 27 60 96. Open: Mon & Wed–Fri 10am–12.30pm & 2–5.30pm, Sat–Sun 2–5.30pm. Closed: Tue. Admission charge. Métro: Rambuteau.

Façade of old café, Musée Carnavalet

Musée de l'Homme

This museum of mankind, housed in the vast Palais de Chaillot, depicts human evolution since the origin of the species, and presents a comparative study of the different races in their traditional environment.

17 place du Trocadéro, 75016. Tel: 01 44 05 72 72. Open: 9.45am–5.15pm. Closed: Tue. Admission charge. Métro: Trocadéro.

Institut du Monde Arabe

The building situated along the river, facing the Ile St-Louis, is the result of close cooperation between France and 19 Arab countries with the aim of promoting cultural exchanges between Islam and the West. The institute houses a reference centre, a video centre, a comprehensive library, research facilities, and a museum (on the 7th floor) that illustrates Arab civilisation from the 9th century onwards. The south façade consists of 1,600 identical metal light screens that electronically filter the sunlight as it enters the building. From the cafeteria on the 9th floor there are lovely views of the river.

1 Rue des Fossés St-Bernard, 75005. Tel: 01 40 51 38 38. www.imarabe.org. Open: 10am–6pm. Closed: Mon. Admission charge. Métro: Jussieu or Cardinal-Lemoine.

Musée Jacquemart André

Situated right in the centre of town, but a little off the visitor's beaten track, this elegant 1870 mansion houses fine collections of Renaissance and 18th-century art, displayed in beautiful surroundings. They include portraits by Gainsborough and Reynolds, paintings and drawings by Rubens, Rembrandt, Van Dyck, Frans Hals and Ruysdaël, 16th-century enamels and ceramics, some beautiful furniture, Beauvais tapestries, and paintings by Boucher and Watteau.

158 boulevard Haussmann, 75008. Tel: 01 45 62 11 59. Open: 10am–6pm. Closed: Mon. Admission charge. Métro: St-Philippe-du-Roule or Miromesnil.

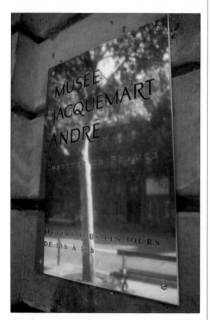

The elegant home of Musée Jacquemart André

Musée de la Marine

Founded in 1827 by Charles X, the museum now occupies the west wing of the Palais de Chaillot. With the help of scale models and actual crafts, it illustrates all kinds of maritime transport from battleships to pleasure boats. There is an interesting royal toy called *Louis XV*, Marie Antoinette's pleasure boat at Versailles, a rowing boat specially built for Napoleon in 1811, and the *Belle Poule* in which his remains were brought back to France from the island of St Helena. The *Gloire*, dating from 1859, was the first armoured warship in the world. And, of course, exhibits include ships used for exploration, such as the *Astrolabe*, which took Dumont d'Urville to the Antarctic in the 19th century, and mementoes of the great explorers La Pérouse, Brazza and Charcot. Temporary exhibitions are a regular feature.

17 Place du Trocadéro, 75016. Tel: 01 53 65 69 69. Open: 10am–6pm. Closed: Tue. Admission charge. Métro: Trocadéro.

Musée Marmottan Monet

This museum has, as a result of various bequests, developed from the original private collection into a museum of Impressionist painting. It bears the name of the art historian Paul Marmottan, who, in 1932, donated his house and private collections to the Académie des Beaux-Arts. These included Renaissance tapestries, furniture and sculpture, as well as early 19th-century paintings and various objets d'art.

Following other legacies, the museum acquired some beautiful medieval manuscripts, and its first Impressionist paintings, including Monet's famous *Impression: Sunrise* (1872), which gave the movement its name.

However, the outstanding asset of the museum is the collection of 65 paintings by Monet donated by his son in 1971.

Ships' figureheads at the Musée de la Marine

Exhibited in a specially built underground gallery, they testify to Monet's love of his country home in Giverny (*see p127*). The different moods of his garden are rendered with supreme mastery. The studies of water lilies, for instance, show the master's obsessive progression towards the huge canvases exhibited in the Orangerie museum (*see p90*).

2 rue Louis-Boilly, 75016. Tel: 01 44 96 50 33. www.marmottan.com. Open: 10am–6pm. Closed: Mon. Admission charge. Métro: La Muette.

Musée du Louvre (*see pp66–7*).
Musée Pierre Marly Lunettes et des Lorgnettes (*see p114*).

Musée de la Musique
See p117.

Musée National de l'Orangerie
The south pavilion on the place de la Concorde houses a substantial collection of paintings from the Impressionist period to the early 20th century, but it is mostly renowned for Monet's *Nymphéas*.

There are some remarkable still lifes by Cézanne, some delightful portraits by Renoir, and paintings by Picasso, Derain, Modigliani and Matisse, as well as a few of Henri Rousseau's best naïve works, including *La Carriole du Père Junier*.

Monet's huge *Nymphéas* (Water Lilies), painted at Giverny, are exhibited on the ground floor in two oval rooms, according to the instructions given by the artist himself. *Place de la Concorde, 75001. Tel: 01 40 05 56 78. www.musee-orangerie.fr. Open: Wed–Mon 12.30–7pm (Fri until 9pm). Closed: Tue. Admission charge. Métro: Concorde.*

Musée National Picasso
The ornate elegance of the 17th-century Hôtel Salé makes a perfect background for the works of a great master of 20th-century art. The building was renovated recently to accommodate a collection of Picasso's works donated to the state by his heirs in lieu of death duties: 200 paintings, more than 150 sculptures, 3,000 drawings and engravings, and 88 ceramics.

Picasso's personal collection of works by other major artists of his time, such as Cézanne, Derain, Braque, Miró, Rousseau and Matisse, was also donated to the state by Jacqueline Picasso.

Picasso's prodigious output is presented in chronological order, starting on the first floor with the 'blue period' (*Autoportrait*), followed by the Cubist period (*Nature morte à la chaise cannée*).

Musée Rodin: works shown outdoors

Pointing the way to that mecca for art lovers – the Musée Picasso

The period between World War I and World War II is illustrated by such paintings as *Paul en arlequin*, *Le Baiser*, *Femme lisant*, and the famous *Portrait de Dora Maar*. Among Picasso's post-war production, the series of studies on Manet's *Déjeuner sur l'Herbe* is particularly remarkable.

Some of Picasso's sculptures are exhibited in the garden, where there is also a pleasant café.

5 rue de Thorigny, 75003. Tel: 01 42 71 25 21. www.musee-picasso.fr. Open: 9.30am–6pm (until 5.30pm winter). Closed: Tue. Admission charge. Métro: St-Paul.

Musée Rodin

The superb collection of Rodin's sculptures is exhibited in the Hôtel Biron, where he lived from 1907 until his death in 1917. Some of his works, in bronze and white marble, are in the house, while others are distributed round the beautiful garden. A visit on a sunny day is highly recommended. In the garden are two of his most famous works: *Le Penseur* and *Les Bourgeois de Calais*, as well as *La Porte de l'Enfer* and *Ugolin*. On the ground floor there are more masterpieces, such as *Le Baiser* and *La Cathédrale*. On the first floor are the plaster casts used for the statues of Balzac and Victor Hugo.

77 rue de Varenne, 75007.
Tel: 01 44 18 61 10. www.musee-rodin.fr.
Open: 9.30am–5.45pm (until 4.45pm winter). Closed: Mon. Admission charge. Métro: Varenne.

Notre-Dame

The harmonious strength of the cathedral's outline, the proportions of its façade, the subtle combination of simplicity and refinement in its design, are undoubtedly the perfect expression of French Gothic architecture. Notre-Dame is the nucleus round which the capital developed, and major celebrations, often marking a turning point in French history, were staged in the cathedral.

One of Notre-Dame's rooftop creatures has the best view in the city

Bishop Maurice de Sully
In 1163, Bishop de Sully launched the building process that lasted nearly 200 years. The architects, Jean de Chelles and Pierre de Montreuil, worked on it during the 13th century, when the Ste-Chapelle was also built. The building was completed in 1345 with the flying buttresses surrounding the chancel.

Notre-Dame today
Although the cathedral never suffered spectacular damage, by the mid-19th century it had been deprived of some of its magnificent sculptures, and the edifice was in serious need of repair. Restoration work was carried out under the care of Viollet-le-Duc, and the cathedral regained its past splendour. Haussmann later widened the Parvis (square) in front of it to increase the dramatic effect of its unique setting.

Today, two other vantage points, the square Jean XXIII behind the chancel, and the square Viviani on the Left Bank, reveal the perfect proportions of the edifice, which is 130m (427ft) long and

49m (161ft) wide. Its towers rise to a height of 68m (223ft).

The façade
The façade is the most striking part of the building. The heavily restored central portal depicts the *Last Judgement*, and the upper part shows Christ surrounded by the celestial court. The portal of the Virgin on the left has a particularly beautiful tympanum illustrating the coronation of the Virgin Mary. The sculptures on the portal of St Anne on the right are the oldest in the cathedral; the remarkable tympanum also shows the Virgin Mary with Bishop Maurice de Sully, founder of the cathedral, at her side. The lintel depicts scenes from the life of St Anne.

The rose window is more than 700 years old. Birds and demons were placed at the base of the towers by Viollet-le-Duc in true Gothic spirit.

The great bell in the south tower, weighing 13 tonnes, is heard only on special occasions. The view from the top is rewarding if you have the courage to climb the 386 steps. The portal on the south side has a 13th-century tympanum, which depicts the martyr St Stephen. The slightly earlier north portal by Jean de Chelles was adorned with a statue of the Virgin and Child, but the child is now missing.

The interior

The vast interior can accommodate up to 9,000 people. The 35-m (115-ft) high nave is separated from the chancel by a wide transept, which has two magnificent rose windows.

The chancel was redecorated in the 17th century as the result of a vow made by Louis XIII if he were granted an heir. A *pietà* by Coysevox stands in the centre, flanked by statues of Louis XIII and Louis XIV. On the right of the chancel, the treasury houses some old relics, including a fragment of the Cross.

Place du Parvis Notre-Dame, 75004. Tel: 01 42 34 56 10. Open: 8am–6.45pm (7.45pm weekends). Métro: St-Michel or Cité. RER: St-Michel-Notre-Dame. Treasury open: 9.30am–6pm Mon–Sat, 2–6pm Sun. Admission charge. Towers open: winter 10am–5.15pm, spring & autumn 9.30am–6pm, 9am–7.30pm in summer (till 11pm weekends). Admission charge for both.

Nearby
Ste-Chapelle, Conciergerie, Churches of St-Julien-le-Pauvre and St-Séverin, Musée Nationale du Moyen Age–Thermes de Cluny, Ile St-Louis.

The cathedral as it appears from the River Seine

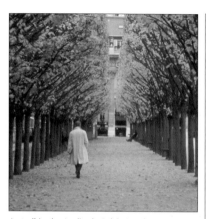

A stroll in the Jardin du Palais-Royal

Opera National de Paris-Garnier

The architecture of this ornately decorated and recently renovated opera house epitomises the elaborate style of the 1860s. It was designed by Charles Garnier, a young and then unknown architect, who was chosen because of the boldness of his plans, which departed from the usual neoclassical style. When the Opéra was inaugurated in 1875, its vast stage, able to accommodate nearly 500 artists, ranked it among the world's finest opera houses.

Groups of statues by various artists welcome visitors at the top of the steps at the main entrance. One of them, *la Danse* by Carpeaux, considered highly risqué when it was created, has been replaced by a copy. The original is in the Musée d'Orsay.

The auditorium, which seats about 2,000, has red and gold as the dominant colours. The ceiling was painted by Chagall during the 1960s. The huge chandelier hanging in the centre weighs nearly 7 tonnes.

Place de l'Opéra, 75002. Tel: 01 40 01 22 63. Open: daily 10am–5pm, except during matinées and special events. Métro: Opéra.

Palais de Chaillot

This site has been much sought-after for its superb views of the river, the Eiffel Tower and the Left Bank. Catherine de Médicis had a country house built on the colline de Chaillot (Chaillot hill).

In 1937, the present building was erected for the Exposition Universelle. Twin pavilions with curved wings are separated by a vast terrace beneath which is the Théâtre National de Chaillot, one of the leading French theatres (entrance through the east pavilion). The palace houses two museums, the Musée de l'Homme and the Musée de la Marine (*see pp88–9*).
Place du Trocadéro, 75016. Métro: Trocadéro.

Palais-Royal

The palace was commissioned in 1624 by Richelieu, who was then Louis XIII's minister. It became a *palais royal* (royal palace) when he left it to the king in his will. Louis XIV then gave it to his brother, Philippe d'Orléans, whose descendants surrounded the garden with elegant shopping arcades and apartments and built the Comédie-Française. Cafés, restaurants, gambling houses and dance halls thrived within its precinct until, in the mid-19th century, Louis-Philippe took the fun out of the area by closing the gambling houses.

The palace is not open to the public, but you can go through the main courtyard, invaded by the black and

white Colonnes de Buren (pillars), into
the peaceful garden surrounded by
dainty boutiques.
Place du Palais-Royal.
Métro: Palais-Royal.

Palais de Tokyo

Situated just upriver from the Palais de
Chaillot, the Palais de Tokyo was also
built for the 1937 world exhibition in
much the same style. It houses the
Musée d'Art Moderne de la Ville de
Paris and a new arts centre (*see p85*).
The surrounding terraces feature
statues by Emile Bourdelle.
*13 avenue du Président-
Wilson, 75016.*
*Métro: Alma-
Marceau.*

The Comédie Française
This famous theatre company was founded
by Louis XIV in 1680, a few years after
Molière's death, with the aim of combining
two rival theatre companies. Frowned upon
by the Sorbonne, it was forced to move
several times, until Napoleon made it an
official institution with a director appointed
by the State. Its repertoire is traditionally
classical, but also includes works by modern
authors, both French and foreign. In the foyer
is the chair that Molière collapsed into during
a performance of *Le Malade Imaginaire*.

A series of pools fronts
the Palais de Chaillot,
across the river from the
Eiffel Tower

Walk: from the Opéra to the Palais-Royal

The prestigious Opéra House and the elegant Palais-Royal epitomise the impression of refinement and grandeur that one gets from this walk.

Allow 2 hours.

Begin from the place de l'Opéra (métro Opéra). Cross the boulevard des Capucines, then turn right.

1 Rue de la Paix

Named rue Napoléon when it was opened in 1806, it is today lined with expensive jewellers (the famous Cartier is at No 13) and has become the symbol of luxury. It leads into the elegant place Vendôme, which Napoleon admires from the top of the central column.

Cross the square, walk along rue de Castiglione and turn left.

2 Rue St-Honoré

The Carré des Feuillants on the corner of the rue de Castiglione is a fashionable but expensive restaurant where you can experiment with *la nouvelle cuisine*. The church of St-Roch halfway down the street stood on a hillock known as the Butte Saint-Roch, which was completely levelled for the building of the avenue de l'Opéra: before that, you had to go down seven steps to gain access to the church; now you have to go up 13.

Further along the street on the right, rue des Pyramides leads to the square which bears the same name, with a gilded statue of Joan of Arc, erected in the 19th century on the very spot where she was wounded while attempting to deliver Paris from English occupation. *Follow rue St-Honoré which leads to the Palais-Royal.*

3 Palais-Royal

As you reach the place André-Malraux, you get a splendid view of the Opéra to your left. Across the square is the Théâtre-Français, home of the famous Comédie-Française (*see pp94–5*). Close by is place Colette, from where you enter the Palais-Royal gardens. Before you do, however, carry on a little further to the Louvre des Antiquaires, which has 250 shops and a convenient restaurant. *Walk through the Jardin du Palais-Royal. Turn right into rue des Petits-Champs and, if you are ready for a meal, try the Mercure Galant at No 15.*

4 Galeries Colbert and Vivienne

These charming covered arcades date from the early 19th century; the Galerie Vivienne is the most beautiful of the two, with its carved, vaulted ceiling and glass roof, and old-fashioned bookshop. *Rue des Petits-Champs leads to the circular place des Victoires with a statue of Louis XIV in the centre (see p109). Leave by rue Vide-Gousset.*

5 Notre-Dame-des-Victoires

The 17th-century church is famous for its paintings, its monument to Lully, and more than 30,000 ex-votos on the walls. *Continue along rue Notre-Dame-des-Victoires, turn left past the Palais de la Bourse (the Stock Exchange), then left again into rue de Richelieu.*

6 Bibliothèque Nationale

Under French law, publishers are required to submit several copies of all works they publish at the Bibliothèque. Since 1992, computerised and multi-media documents are also required to be submitted. To help house this exhaustive collection, a new facility has been built at the quai François Mitterand site in the 13th *arrondissement*.

7 Fontaine Molière

Further along rue de Richelieu, you will see a 19th-century fountain, dedicated to Molière, not far from the house (now No 40) where he died in 1673 after collapsing on stage. *Turn right into rue Thérèse, then follow rue Ste-Anne back to rue des Petits-Champs; on the corner stands Lully's house adorned with musical motives. Walk back along avenue de l'Opéra.*

Nearby
Musée Grévin, La Madeleine, Palais du Louvre, Jardin des Tuileries.

The Panthéon

This vast monument towering over the Latin Quarter tends to dwarf everything around it, particularly the beautiful church of St-Etienne-du-Mont. Looked at from a distance, however, the harmonious proportions of its high dome, underlined by an elegant ring of slender columns, make it a splendid example of neoclassical architecture.

In 1791, the Assemblée Constituante decided that all the nation's 'great men' should be buried inside the church, which was renamed Panthéon after the Greek and Roman temples dedicated to all the gods. However, with the return of the monarchy, the building became a church once again until, in 1885, the decision was finally taken to restore it to its role of national mausoleum, in honour of the writer Victor Hugo who had just died.

The Panthéon, where the illustrious rest

The interior

Forty-two of the original windows were blocked up in 1791 and the bare walls were later decorated with scenes depicting the life of St Geneviève by Pierre Puvis de Chavannes, as well as paintings by other late 19th-century artists.

In the vast crypt are the tombs of some of France's 'great men': Voltaire, Rousseau, Hugo, Zola, the Resistance leader Jean Moulin, Jean Monnet, usually referred to as the 'father of Europe', and many others.
Place du Panthéon, 75005.
Tel: 01 44 32 18 00. Open: daily 10am–6.30pm. Admission charge. Métro: Cardinal-Lemoine. RER: Luxembourg.

St Geneviève Church

When, in 1744, Louis XV suffered a serious illness, he vowed to build a beautiful new church to replace the ancient church of St Geneviève Abbey. After his recovery, he commissioned the architect, Jacques Soufflot, who designed a magnificent building in the shape of a Greek cross, with a huge dome 83m (272ft) high; the saint's shrine would be placed beneath it. Work began in 1758, but was only completed after Soufflot's death in 1789, on the eve of the French Revolution.

Place des Vosges

This beautiful square is a refreshing haven compared with the magnificent place de la Concorde or the supremely elegant place Vendôme. Its sober yet extremely refined architecture gives it a kind of exquisite charm.

Victor Hugo's house, place des Vosges

Commissioned by Henri IV at the beginning of the 17th century, the square was inaugurated after his death by his son Louis XIII and named place Royale. The two higher buildings, in the centre of the south and north sides, are called Pavillon du Roi (King's Pavilion) and Pavillon de la Reine (Queen's Pavilion) respectively, though they were never inhabited by the royal family. In the central garden stands a statue of Louis XIII. The square was renamed place des Vosges in 1800.

Some of the other residences have been lived in by famous people: Madame de Sévigné was born at No 1 bis in 1626, Cardinal Richelieu occupied No 21 before he moved to the Palais-Royal, and Victor Hugo lived in No 6 from 1832 to 1848, before his exile to Jersey and Guernsey. The house is now a museum with various mementoes of his life: furniture, objects he collected, portraits and photographs, and also drawings by Hugo himself.

Maison de Victor Hugo, 6 place des Vosges, 75004. Tel: 01 42 72 10 16. Open: Tue–Sun 10am–5.40pm. Closed: Mon. Permanent collection: admission free. Admission charge for temporary exhibitions. Métro: St-Paul.

Place Vendôme

Built at the end of the 17th century by Jules Hardouin-Mansart, this imposing square is a magnificent example of the Louis XIV style.

Here again, symmetry is the overriding principle: a terrace of mansions over a row of arcades, with an original feature designed to break the monotony. The central buildings and those cutting the four corners are surmounted by pediments. Chopin died at No 12, and No 15 is now the prestigious Ritz Hotel; famous jewellers are established all round the square.

The central column that replaced the equestrian statue of Louis XIV was erected by Napoleon to celebrate his victory at Austerlitz.

The statue at the top was changed many times until the Third Republic finally settled on a copy of the original, representing Napoleon dressed as a Roman (*see p96*).
Métro: Tuileries or Opéra.

Les Quais

The *quais* (embankments) are the city's main thoroughfares, carrying fast-moving traffic from east to west and vice versa. Lined with wide pavements planted with trees, the *quais* offer lovely walks along the river with fine views of the monuments situated on both banks of the Seine and on the Ile-de-la-Cité:

The Right Bank

The quai de la Mégisserie and the quai de Gesvres are lined with picturesque pet shops. From here there is a splendid view across the river of the Conciergerie on the Ile-de-la-Cité. The tiny square de l'Ave Maria offers an interesting view of the medieval Hôtel de Sens. Across the Pont Marie is the Ile St-Louis.

The Left Bank

There are striking views of Notre-Dame from the quai de la Tournelle, and from the quai de Montebello; just off the latter is the delightful square René-Viviani. Past the place St-Michel, the quai des Grands-Augustins, named after a nearby monastery, is lined with second-hand bookstalls on the riverside, and has several 17th-century mansions on the other side. The Pont-Neuf, the oldest bridge in Paris, is in two sections, joining the Right and Left Banks to the Ile-de-la-Cité.
Métro: Pont-Neuf, Châtelet, Pont Marie & St-Michel.

Sacré-Coeur

Visible from almost anywhere in Paris, the white basilica has become one of the city's most famous landmarks (*see p77*). The decision to build it was taken by the Assemblée Nationale in 1873, to boost public morale after the Franco-Prussian War. Work started in 1875, but the building was only completed in 1914, and consecrated after World War I. The architecture is a bit disappointing, but its Byzantine basilica makes it highly visible on the skyline. The mosaic decorating the chancel vaulting is impressive. It is possible to go up to the top of the dome for a superb view of Paris.
Parvis du Sacré-Coeur, 75018. Tel: 01 53 41 89 00. Basilica open: daily 6am–10.30pm. Dome and crypt open: 9.30am–7pm summer, 10am–5.30pm winter. Admission charge to crypt and dome. Métro: Anvers, then access by funicular.

Ste-Chapelle

The distinctive, 75-m (246-ft) high spire in the sky reveals from a distance the presence of this jewel of Gothic architecture, partly hidden by the Palais de Justice buildings. In 1239, Louis IX, better known as St-Louis,

LES BOUQUINISTES

Second-hand bookstalls are one of the familiar sights of Paris, and a stroll along the river would be less enjoyable without them. The tattered, green-painted boxes that used to be carried to and fro by their owners have become permanent fixtures. At night they are locked, but in the afternoon they open one by one, like stranded sea shells, revealing books, prints, postcards and maps. A browse under their precariously propped-up lids is always fun, although there are not many rare editions or bargains to be found in them any more.

acquired the Crown of Thorns from the Emperor of Constantinople, together with other precious relics, including a fragment of the True Cross, and immediately decided to build a special shrine to house them in the courtyard of the royal palace. Pierre de Montreuil was entrusted with this delicate task. The Ste-Chapelle was built in less than three years and consecrated in 1248. After the Revolution, it was no longer used as a church, and the relics were transferred to Notre-Dame where they are now kept in the Treasury.

In order to let in as much light as possible, the vaulted roof was supported by thin pillars which were separated by long, narrow stained-glass windows 15m (49ft) high. A few buttresses help reinforce the structure,

which appears to have no walls. The narrow edifice consists of two chapels, one above the other. The *chapelle basse* (lower chapel) is richly decorated, and its floor paved with tombstones. A spiral staircase leads to the *chapelle haute* (upper chapel), which appears wrapped in a blaze of light and colour. The huge stained-glass windows are undoubtedly the most striking feature: still mainly 13th-century, they are the oldest in Paris, depicting over 1,000 scenes from the Old and New Testaments in great detail.

4 boulevard du Palais, 75004. Tel: 01 53 73 78 50. Open: daily, summer 9.30am–6pm, winter 10am–5pm. Admission charge. Access through the Cour de Mai of the Palais de Justice. Métro: St-Michel or Cité.

The Sacré-Coeur, today a city landmark

Walk: Rive Droite, Rive Gauche

This takes you from the 'royal' Tuileries Gardens across the river to the Faubourg St-Germain, once fashionable with the aristocracy, whose splendid mansions have now been taken over by ministries and embassies.

Allow 2 hours (excluding visit to Musée d'Orsay).

1 Rue de Rivoli

The elegant arcades, once lined with smart boutiques, now house souvenir shops. The hotel Meurice, at No 228, served as headquarters of the German high command during World War II.
Enter the Tuileries Gardens on your right.

2 Jardin des Tuileries

Laid out in 1664 by Louis XIV's chief gardener, André Le Nôtre, the gardens soon became a popular place for strolling. The western end is quite elaborate, with its octagonal pool surrounded by statues, terraces and twin pavilions, while from the round pool at the other end, the view extends all the way to the Champs Elysées and the Arc de Triomphe.
The Terrasse du Bord de l'Eau, by the river, affords good views of the Left Bank. Cross the Pont de Solferino.

3 Palais de la Légion d'Honneur

Take rue de la Légion d'Honneur between the impressive Musée d'Orsay (to the left), which has a convenient restaurant, and the Musée National de la Légion d'Honneur (to the right) which illustrates the history of the orders of French Chivalry before the 1789 Revolution, and the Legion of Honour, which Napoleon founded in 1802.
Tel: 01 40 62 84 25. Open: Tue–Sun 2–5pm. Closed: Mon.
Turn left into rue de Lille. Rue de Poitiers leads to the rue de l'Université. On reaching the boulevard St-Germain, turn left, then turn left again into rue du Bac.

4 St-Thomas-d'Aquin

Begun in the 17th century and finished in the 18th, this church, on the left, was originally the chapel of a Dominican monastery. Inside are some fine 17th- and 18th-century paintings, which provide a perfect setting for the regular Sunday organ concerts.

Follow rue de Luynes to rue de Grenelle, and turn right past the elaborate Fontaine des Quatre Saisons (see p53). Turn left.

5 Rue de Varenne

The name of the street is derived from *gerenne* (warren), a reminder of the days when Faubourg was a rural area. It is lined with several stately mansions: the most famous is the Hôtel Matignon at No 57, the prime minister's official residence since 1958. Built in 1721 and once owned by Talleyrand, it has the largest private gardens in Paris. Its contemporary, the Hôtel Biron at the end of the street, also has beautiful gardens. Today the building houses a museum dedicated to the sculptor Rodin, who lived there.

Turn right, then right again into rue de Grenelle, taking a look at the smaller-scale Hôtel de Lillars at No 118.

6 Palais Bourbon

The rue de Bellechasse and the boulevard St-Germain bring you back to the river, past the impressive Palais Bourbon (seat of the Assemblée Nationale), remodelled by Napoleon to match the Madeleine facing it on the other side of the place de la Concorde.

Cross the Pont de la Concorde and the place de la Concorde, then follow rue Royale towards the Madeleine.

Nearby
Rue du Faubourg-St-Honoré, Place Vendôme, Invalides, Pont Alexandre.

Striking sculptural art provides an added attraction in the elegant Jardin des Tuileries

The classical façade of La Madeleine as viewed from La Concorde

St-Germain-des-Prés

Situated on the Left Bank, in the Latin Quarter, St-Germain-des-Prés has, since the days of Sartre and the Existentialists, been known as the rallying place of the intellectual avant-garde, who traditionally met in the literary cafés of the boulevard St-Germain.

The district nestles round the ancient church of St-Germain-des-Prés (*see p41*) and abounds in interesting contrasts. The wide boulevard St-Germain, cutting right across it and carrying fast traffic eastwards, spoils the immediate surroundings of the church a bit, but the backstreets are delightful, each having its own attractive feature. There is the rue de Buci with its lively open-air market, and the very old streets in the vicinity of the quaint place de Fürstemberg, rue Cardinale, rue de l'Echaudé, going back to the 14th century, and rue Bourbon-le-Château.

Further west, rue Bonaparte and rue des Sts-Pères, running down to the river, are lined with old-fashioned antique shops and art galleries, while rue Jacob, at right angles to them, is one of the most pleasant streets in the area. On the busy boulevard St-Germain, near the place St-Germain-des-Prés, are the well-known cafés closely associated with the district, the Café des Deux Magots and the Café de Flore. *Métro: St-Germain-des-Prés or Mabillon.*

Ste-Marie Madeleine

This church in the guise of a Greek temple is known

(see p41)

LITERARY CAFÉS

Several cafés near the church of St-Germain-des-Prés have been the rendezvous of intellectuals and artists. The Procope, rue de l'Ancienne-Comédie, just off the Carrefour de l'Odéon, is the oldest. It was opened in 1686, by a Sicilian whose excellent coffee drew actors from the Comédie-Française opposite. Later, it attracted philosophers such as Voltaire and Rousseau, revolutionaries like Danton, Robespierre and Marat, and famous 19th-century writers and poets, Musset, George Sand, Balzac and Hugo. The claim to fame of the Flore and the Deux Magots is much more recent. In the late 1940s and 1950s, they became the haunt of Sartre, Simone de Beauvoir, Camus, Prévert, and the post-war generation of philosophers and poets. They are still favoured by today's intellectuals, but the magic has gone.

Tête-à-tête, boulevard St-Germain

to Parisians simply as La Madeleine. Two partly erected churches were successively razed before Napoleon had this temple built in honour of his Grande Armée. It was completed only in 1842, and by then it had been decided that the temple would be a church.

Fifty-two massive Corinthian columns surround the building, which dominates the centre of the place de la Madeleine with its flower market and well-known luxury delicatessens, Hédiard and Fauchon. Inside the church are some interesting 19th-century sculptures, including *Le Baptême du Christ* by François Rude, and *Le Mariage de la Vierge* by Pradier.

Place de la Madeleine, 75008.
Tel: 01 44 51 69 00. Open: daily 7.30am–7pm. Métro: Madeleine.

Les Deux Magots, a café frequented by post-war philosophers and poets such as Jean-Paul Sartre

Walk: St-Germain-des-Prés

Literary cafés, jazz cellars, informal bistros, bookshops, fashion boutiques and antique shops, as well as one of the oldest churches in Paris, are the main attractions here. *Allow 2 hours.*

Start from the Odéon métro station.

1 Carrefour de l'Odéon

Cross over the boulevard St-Germain: No 130 marks the entrance of the Cour du Commerce St-André. This alleyway and covered arcade has revolutionary associations: Marat's newspaper, *l'Ami du Peuple*, was printed at No 8, and it was here that Dr Guillotin's deadly invention was first tested on sheep. On your right, enter the picturesque courtyards of the Cour de Rohan. *Retrace your steps and turn right.*

Relaxing by a floral forest

2 Rue de l'Ancienne Comédie

The most prestigious theatre company in France, the Comédie-Française, performed at No 14 until 1770. The Café Procope opposite has, since 1686, been the meeting place of writers, politicians and philosophers (*see p104*). *Follow rue Dauphine to the embankment, and turn left.*

3 Monnaie de Paris (Mint)

This late 18th-century building houses the Musée de la Monnaie. Displays include tools, presses and drawings. *Tel: 01 40 46 55 35. Open: Tue–Fri 11am–5.30pm. Weekends noon–5.30pm. Closed: Mon. Admission charge. Continue along quai de Conti to the place de l'Institut.*

4 Institut de France

The 17th-century domed building by Le Vau houses the Bibliothèque Mazarin, including Cardinal Mazarin's own collection of rare books. Since 1805, it has also housed the Institut de France, founded during the 1789 Revolution. It includes the Académie Française, set up by Richelieu in 1635. *Turn left into rue Bonaparte; on the right is the Ecole des Beaux Arts (Academy of Art), visible from the courtyard.*

5 Rues des Beaux-Arts, Visconti and Jacob

The whole area had many famous inhabitants including Oscar Wilde, Jean Racine, Honoré de Balzac, Eugène Delacroix and Camille Corot. The rue de Seine is lined with art galleries, and rue Jacob has many antique shops and several quiet hotels. Nearby is rue de Buci, with its well-known street market.

From rue Jacob turn right into rue de Fürstemberg.

6 Place de Fürstemberg

This charming little square seems to belong to another time and place: it looks delightfully provincial with its romantic catalpa trees and old-fashioned street lamps. Delacroix had his studio at No 6; this is now a national museum with mementoes of the artist.
Open: daily 9.30am–5pm. Closed: Tue. Rue de l'Abbaye brings you back to rue Bonaparte; turn left. The church of St-Germain-des-Prés was once part of a powerful abbey. Close by is the wide boulevard St-Germain.

7 Literary Landmarks

Immediately on your right is the Café des Deux Magots and, almost next door, the Café de Flore, where intellectuals and artists have been meeting for generations. It is a good spot to get the feel of the area over a cup of coffee. The Brasserie Lipp opposite is a rather more select rendezvous for celebrities.
Continue up rue Bonaparte, then turn left into rue St-Sulpice. Pass the church and turn right along rue de Tournon.

8 Luxembourg

Marie de Médicis, widow of Henri IV, had the palace modelled on the Palazzo Pitti in Florence. It is now the seat of the Sénat. The gardens are adorned with numerous statues and the famous Fontaine de Médicis (*see p52*).
Coming out of the gardens, follow rue Rotrou to the 18th-century place de l'Odéon. Rue Crébillon and rue Condé take you back to the Carrefour de l'Odéon.

Nearby
Rue St-André-des-Arts, Rue de Buci market.

Streets and squares

Elegant streets and popular ones, imposing squares and tiny, quaint ones, all reflect the life of the city, in turn quiet and bustling, hurried and leisurely.

The famous logo of a popular restaurant

Rue Mouffetard

Running downhill from the top of the Montagne Ste-Geneviève, rue Mouffetard (the 'Mouff') is one of the most picturesque streets in Paris. The bottom section is the liveliest, with its open-air market, the colourful shop signs creating a village-like atmosphere. A little way up, on either side, are the passage des Postes and the passage des Patriarches, both worth exploring, while further up still, on the left, the rue du Pot-de-Fer has some interesting restaurants. The Fontaine du Pot-de-Fer, on the corner, was built in the 17th century and supplied by an aqueduct that brought water to the Palais du Luxembourg. The street ends at the charming place de la Contrescarpe. *75005. Métro: Monge or Censier-Daubenton.*

Rue Quincampoix

Situated near the Centre Pompidou, this old street was the scene, in 1720, of a famous scandal involving the Scottish financier, John Law. He founded a bank, encouraged wild speculation, and the inevitable crash ruined thousands. There are some interesting old houses near the junction with rue des Lombards. *75004. Métro: Châtelet or Rambuteau.*

The lively, open-air market charms visitors to the rue Mouffetard

Rue Royale

This elegant street, which links the place de la Concorde and the Madeleine, has wide pavements lined with luxury shops.

Near the place de la Concorde, Maxim's is still one of the leading restaurants of the capital.

75008. Métro: Concorde or Madeleine.

Rue St-André-des-Arts

Going west towards St-Germain-des-Prés from the Latin Quarter, the rue St-André-des-Arts is popular with young people and tourists enjoying the incessant animation around the cafés, crêperies, snack bars, souvenir shops and bookshops.

The Cour du Commerce St-André on the left is an 18th-century arcade lined with shops and cafés with picturesque old beams.

75006. Métro: St-Michel.

Place du Châtelet

This was extensively remodelled by Haussmann, who commissioned two theatres from the architect Davioud: the Théâtre du Châtelet, where musicals, operas and concerts are still regularly staged, and the Théâtre de la Ville, once the Théâtre Sarah Bernhardt, where the famous actress delighted Parisians with her inspired performances.

75001. Métro: Châtelet.

Place Emile-Goudeau

This unpretentious square, where the famous Bateau-Lavoir building (*see p78*) once stood, still possesses some of the old magic of Montmartre.

75018. Métro: Abbesses.

Meridian Line, St-Sulpice

Place de l'Odéon

The square has hardly altered since the late 18th century. The sober architecture of its houses contrasts with the Greek-temple style of the Théâtre National de l'Odéon dating from 1782. The Café Voltaire at No 1 was the meeting place of 18th-century philosophers, including Voltaire, Diderot and d'Alembert. It no longer exists.

75006. Métro: Odéon.

Place St-Sulpice

Dominated by its monumental fountain (*see p53*) and the twin-towered church of St-Sulpice (*see p43*), this square is an ideal place for a pause while visiting the St-Germain-des-Prés area.

75006. Métro: St-Sulpice or Mabillon.

Place des Victoires

The original statue of Louis XIV was installed by a rich admirer of the king, who subsequently had the square designed by Mansart to match the statue. Recently renovated, the square has attracted several well-known fashion boutiques.

75002. Métro: Bourse or Palais-Royal.

Tour Eiffel

Its spindly greyish figure has been painted, photographed, joked about, written and sung about more than any other monument in Paris, and today, after more than 100 years, the Eiffel Tower still retains the key to its initial success: instant appeal. Once your curiosity is roused, it will continue to grow as you get closer, and you will never be disappointed, for it is a strange monument indeed, with its graceful outline, combined with the huge steel struts that are locked together in an intricate web.

Scientific and artistic challenge

It is no surprise that the idea for such a daring project should have come from a

Once vilified on aesthetic grounds, now a favourite subject of artists

group of engineers, headed by Gustave Eiffel, working on steel bridges and viaducts. Plans submitted by Maurice Koechlin and Emile Nouguier won first prize in a competition organised for the 1889 Exposition Universelle, and Gustave Eiffel exclaimed enthusiastic-ally: 'France will be the only nation with a 300m flagstaff!'

Built in record time

The tower was completed by 300 workers in just over two years from January 1887 to March 1889. This was made possible by the extreme precision of the plans, which gave the exact measurements for over 12,000 metallic parts. Two-and-a-half-million rivets were used and, when it was inaugurated, it was the tallest building in the world.

For and against

The tower's success was immediate. During the six months of the exhibition, nearly 2 million visitors came to see the 'iron lady' and, by the end of the year, three-quarters of the building cost had

Queuing to climb the 1,710 steps to the top

already been recovered. The tower may have had its fans, but it also had its critics. Three hundred writers and artists signed a protest addressed to the municipality, qualifying it as 'useless and monstrous'.

A narrow escape

Concession had been granted to keep the structure standing for 20 years only, and the tower was due to be pulled down in 1909.

However, by then it was playing an essential role in the rapidly developing world of telecommunications. It was saved, and proved to be an indispensable asset in establishing the first radio telephone service across the Atlantic, and as a meteorological station. In 1957, its height increased by another 20m (66ft) when a television transmitter was fitted at the top. In preparation for its hundredth anniversary, it was given a new look and completely repainted, and glitters elegantly now under more powerful lights.

The climb

A visit to the viewing platforms is a must. The view from the top floor is breathtaking, and can extend as far as 67km (42 miles) in exceptional weather conditions. If you wait until late afternoon on a clear day the sun has had time to disperse all signs of morning mist. You will almost certainly have to queue for the lifts, as the tower is very popular. On your way up, you may wish to stop on the first floor where there is a free video show on the history of the building.

Champ de Mars, 75007.
Tel: 01 44 11 23 23. www.tour-eiffel.fr.
Open: 9.30am–11pm (9am–midnight in summer). Admission charge.
Métro: Trocadéro or Bir-Hakeim.
RER: Champ-de-Mars-Tour-Eiffel.

Nearby
Jardins du Trocadéro, Palais de Chaillot and its museums, Musée des Arts Asiatiques-Guimet, Musée d'Art Moderne de la Ville de Paris.

Unknown Paris

Paris is more than breathtaking vistas, impressive monuments, or the glamour associated with the Champs-Elysées–Madeleine–Opéra districts. It can also be seen at a more leisurely pace along a canal, or in a hidden museum, in an arcade, or even in a cemetery.

Millions of skeletons lie in the Catacombs

Underground Paris

The city's network of tunnels has many practical uses other than the métro, and part of it can be visited. In the 18th century, Parisians found a new use for some underground galleries on the site of Roman stone quarries. They became a much-needed cemetery to relieve the overcrowded Cimetière des Innocents situated near Les Halles, where the Fontaine des Innocents now stands. The site was consecrated, and the bones were piled along the galleries. There are now guided visits to these catacombs.
Les Catacombes, 1 place Denfert-Rochereau, 75014. Tel: 01 43 22 47 63. Open: Tue–Sun 10am–6pm. Closed: Mon. Admission charge. Métro: Denfert-Rochereau.

Les Egouts (the sewers) formed part of the modernisation programme that was undertaken by Baron Haussmann in the 19th century, with the network totalling some 2,000km (1,250 miles). The visit includes the showing of a video film which explains how the whole system works.
Place de la Résistance, 75007. Tel: 01 53 68 27 81. Open: 11am–4pm (5pm in summer). Closed: Thur & Fri. Admission charge. Métro: Alma-Marceau.

Along the Canal St-Martin

The Canal St-Martin was dug in the early 19th century to link the Canal de l'Ourcq, running eastwards from La Villette, and the Seine. It winds its way across the eastern districts of Paris over a distance of 4.5km (2³/₄ miles) and joins the river just south of the Bastille.

The most picturesque section lies between rue du Faubourg du Temple and rue Louis Blanc. The most relaxing way to enjoy the canal is to take a three-hour cruise from the Musée d'Orsay to La Villette. (*See* Organised Tours, *p186*.)

For those who prefer to walk beside the canal, the best way is to start either from the place de la République (*métro: République*) or the place de Stalingrad (*métro: Stalingrad or Jaurès*).

Arcades

Covered arcades were in fashion at the end of the 18th and at the beginning of the 19th century. Some of them, like the Galerie Vivienne (*see p97*), were elaborately decorated. Called *galeries* or *passages*, they are today lined with boutiques. The best are between rue de Rivoli and the Grands Boulevards, west of the boulevard de Sébastopol. The following should not be missed:

Galerie Vivienne *4 place des Petits-Champs, 75002. Métro: Bourse.*
Passage Choiseul *44 rue des Petits-Champs, 75002. Métro: Quatre-Septembre.*
Passage des Princes *97 rue de Richelieu, 75002. Métro: Richelieu-Drouot.*
Passage des Panoramas *11 boulevard Montmartre, 75009. Métro: Grands Boulevards.*
Passage Jouffroy *10 boulevard Montmartre, 75009. Métro: Grands Boulevards.*
Passage Verdeau *31 bis rue du Faubourg-Montmartre, 75009. Métro: Le Peletier.*
Passage du Caire *2 place du Caire, 75002. Métro: Sentier.*
Galerie Vérot-Dodat *19 rue Jean-Jacques Rousseau, 75001. Métro: Palais-Royal.*

Cimetière du Père-Lachaise
This is Paris's largest cemetery. A plan is available at the main entrance to help you locate the graves of the famous: Alfred de Musset was buried beneath a weeping willow; the tragic lovers Héloïse and Abélard (*see p60*) are buried here; so are Oscar Wilde and Molière, Baron Haussmann, actress Sarah Bernhardt, singer Edith Piaf, and others.
Main entrance from boulevard de Ménil-montant, 75020. Open: daily 8.30am–6pm. Métro: Père-Lachaise.

On the east side of the cemetery is the old village of **Charonne**. Its medieval church of St-Germain-de-Charonne is surrounded by a tiny cemetery, and its high street, rue St-Blaise, is lined with small houses. The area has managed to retain its village atmosphere despite being close to the high-rise buildings of Belleville and Ménilmontant.
Métro: Gambetta.

Musée Cernuschi
The house and personal collection of Oriental art of banker Henri Cernuschi form the basis of this museum, bequeathed to the city of Paris before his death in 1896. Ancient Chinese art, including neolithic terracottas, is particularly well represented.
7 avenue Vélasquez, 75008. Tel: 01 45 63 50 75. Open: 10am–5.40pm. Closed: Mon. Admission charge. Métro: Monceau or Villiers.

Musée de la Magie
This museum of magic and curiosities spreads through several cellar-like rooms and is great fun for children and adults alike. Live magic shows and a wonderful shop.
11 rue St Paul, 75004. Tel: 01 42 72 13 26. www.museedelamagie.com. Open: Wed, Sat & Sun 2–7pm. Admission charge. Métro: St Paul.

Edith Piaf's tomb, Père-Lachaise cemetery

Musée Pierre Marly Lunettes et des Lorgnettes

The history of spectacles and various kinds of glasses, such as opera and fieldglasses, is depicted by means of many fascinating exhibits, sometimes elaborately decorated.

380 rue St Honoré, 75008. Tel: 01 40 20 06 98. Open: Tue–Sat 10am–noon, 2–6pm. Closed: Sun, Mon & Aug. Métro: Concorde.

Musée Nissim de Camondo

This private mansion backing on to the Parc Monceau was donated to the nation by the Comte de Camondo. It recreates the interior of an elegant 18th-century house with furniture made by the most famous cabinetmakers, and with Beauvais tapestries, precious ornaments and china.

63 rue Monceau, 75008. Tel: 01 53 89 06 50. Open: 10am–5.30pm. Closed: Mon & Tue. Admission charge. Métro: Villiers or Monceau.

Musée Dapper

The first museum in Paris dedicated entirely to Africa – ancient and modern – displays excellent wood statues and masks, bronzes, historical paintings and prints, as well as receptacles, textiles and jewellery. The wood-panelled hall is a fine setting for lively displays of music, dance and theatre.

35 rue Paul Valéry, 75116. Tel: 01 45 00 01 50. Open: daily except Tue 11am–7pm. Admission charge. Métro: Victor Hugo.

Nouvelle Athènes

Situated south of the place Pigalle, this district owes its romantic name partly

Fine artworks at the Musée Gustave Moreau

to the neoclassical architecture of its houses, and partly to the fact that, in the early 18th century, it attracted the artistic and intellectual elite of the capital, and rivalled the Faubourg St-Germain.

Musée de la Vie Romantique

Housed in the former home of the painter Ary Scheffer, the museum is devoted to the artists and writers who used to be his regular guests: George Sand, Chopin, Delacroix, Liszt, Dickens, Turgenev, and many others.

16 rue Chaptal, 75009. Tel: 01 48 74 95 38. Open: 10am–6pm. Closed: Mon. Admission charge. Métro: St-Georges or Pigalle.

Musée Gustave Moreau

Another 19th-century painter's house has been turned into a museum. Moreau's symbolism influenced his famous pupils at the Ecole des Beaux-Arts, Rouault and Matisse.

14 rue de la Rochefoucauld, 75009. Tel: 01 48 74 38 50. Open: daily, except

Tue, 10am–12.45pm & 2–5.15pm.
Admission charge. Métro: Trinité or
St-Georges.

Passy

Annexed to the city of Paris in 1860, the 'village' of Passy is today a much sought-after residential district in the western part of the capital.

Maison de Balzac

This museum is devoted to the 19th-century novelist who depicted French society with such mastery. It contains manuscripts, caricatures and engravings. Balzac lived here for seven years and regularly evaded his creditors by slipping out through the back entrance in the cobbled rue Berton.
47 rue Raynouard, 75016. Tel: 01 55 74 41 80. Open: 10am–6pm. Closed: Mon. Admission charge. Métro: Passy.
RER: Kennedy-Radio-France.

Musée du Vin

The museum has found an apt home in the ancient cellars of the 15th-century former Passy Monastery; wine-tasting is included in the visit.
Rue des Eaux, 75016. Tel: 01 45 25 63 26.
www.museeduvinparis.com. Open:
Tue–Sun 10am–6pm. Closed: Mon.
Admission charge. Métro: Passy.

Temple

This district south of the place de la République was named after the Knights Templars. In 1808 the site became an open-air second-hand clothes market known as the Carreau du Temple; the clothes were laid directly on the pavement. Today, cheap clothes are sold in a covered market, but the site has retained its picturesque name.
Métro: Temple.

Val-de-Grâce

The buildings of the former abbey are situated on the edge of the Latin Quarter. Mansart designed the church in the Jesuit style fashionable at that time, with a two-tier façade, a dome modelled on St Peter's in Rome and, above all, superb baroque decorations. Particularly remarkable are the huge baldachin resting on six twisted columns, and the painting in the cupola by Pierre Mignard. Following the Revolution, the abbey became a military hospital.
Rue St-Jacques (boulevard de Port-Royal end), 75005.
RER: Port-Royal or Luxembourg.

Val-de-Grâce

La Villette

The vast complex of La Villette has been developed on both sides of the canal de l'Ourcq, between the Porte de la Villette and the Porte de Pantin. Buildings on the original site have been incorporated into the project. The object of building a major new cultural centre on the edge of the city was to revive interest in this long-neglected eastern district, while taking advantage of the enormous amount of space that was available.

Futuristic design at
La Villette

Cité des Sciences et de l'Industrie

Inaugurated in 1986, the complex has already proved very successful, attracting an increasing number of visitors of all ages. Much more than a museum, it is a constantly updated reference centre, keeping track of the rapid evolution of science and technology. Its novelty lies in the fact that visitors are encouraged to take part in various projects and demonstrations. This makes it a realistic and entertaining study centre, particularly suitable for children.

The building itself, incorporating a former 19th-century auction hall, was designed by Fainsilber, who used the reflection of light off the steel-and-glass structure to achieve futuristic effects. The glass reveals mechanisms usually kept hidden, as in the main escalators or the glasshouses on the south façade.
Parc de la Villette, 30 avenue Corentin-Cariou, 75019. Tel: 01 40 05 12 12. Open: 10am–6pm (7pm on Sun). Closed: Mon. Admission charge; headsets for audio tour of Explora *in English can be hired. Métro: Porte-de-la-Villette or Corentin-Cariou.*

Explora

This permanent exhibition, staged on three levels and including tours, activities and workshops, illustrates four broad themes:

The **Earth and the Universe** deals with the exploration of the oceans, the geological history of the earth, movements of the continents, travel and experiments in space. The Planetarium aims to explain the complexity of the universe with programmes such as 'Life and Death of a Star' and 'Space Oasis'. **The Adventure of Life** deals with the human environment, man and the secrets of life. **Man and Matter** is concerned with man's control of energy and other resources, transport and economic trends. **Language and Communications** covers the world of sounds and images and various aspects of man's social behaviour.

The centre also includes a fully computerised, multimedia library with special material available for children (*la Médiathèque*), a cinema showing documentaries and fiction films to introduce viewers to the world of science (*le Cinéma Louis-Lumière*), and two discovery areas for children aged 3 to 6 and 6 to 12 years (*l'Inventorium*).

La Géode

This shiny steel globe, close to the main building, acts as a vast mirror, reflecting the surroundings and the changing sky with great intensity. The auditorium has a 1,000-sq m (10,764-sq ft) hemispheric screen. Films on scientific subjects are shown throughout the day.

The Maison de la Villette, housed in the recently renovated Rotonde des Vétérinaires, has an exhibition of local history. The park extends across the canal de l'Ourcq: green open spaces, with red *folies* (follies) dotted about. These are see-through cubical pavilions, varying in shape and used for practical purposes. There is a children's centre, information centre, video studios, café and first-aid centre. The Grande Halle, dating from 1867, is an iron structure that was a cattle market until the 1970s. It is now a venue for exhibitions and trade fairs. The **Zénith** is a vast hall that has the capacity to accommodate approximately 6,500 spectators and is used mainly for rock concerts.

The **Cité de la Musique** is the other main complex in the park. The home of the Conservatoire National Supérieur de Musique, the higher national music academy, it houses a concert hall and the **Musée de la Musique**.

La Géode: film shows are every hour 10.30am–8.30pm. Admission charge.
Cité de la Musique: 221 avenue Jean-Jaurès, 75019. Métro: Porte de Pantin.
Musée de la Musique: Open: noon–6pm (10am–6pm Sun). Closed: Mon. Admission charge.

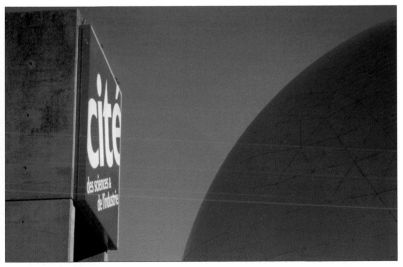

The spectacular Géode dominates this family-friendly complex and park

Paris environs

La Défense

This entirely modern district lies to the west of Paris, across the Pont de Neuilly. A statue in the central square, symbolising the defence of Paris during the Franco-Prussian war of 1871, gives the area its name.

Bold town planning

Town planners had been toying for a long time with the idea of extending the Voie Triomphale. This broad avenue, designed by Le Nôtre in the 17th century, sweeps across the city in a straight line from the Louvre to the Arc de Triomphe.

Development began in the late 1950s, and architects experimented with new ideas. One of the driving principles was the total separation of pedestrian and motorised traffic. The vast complex is surrounded by a *boulevard circulaire* (ring road) carrying through-traffic, with underground link roads and outlets leading to specific areas at different levels.

A broad pedestrian avenue, called the Esplanade du Général de Gaulle, rises in steps from the Seine and gives access to the various groups of buildings: a variety of towers housing offices, a few blocks of flats, a vast shopping complex called Les Quatre-Temps, and the CNIT (Centre National des Industries et des Techniques), the oldest building on the site. Its concrete shell, resting on just three supports, was considered revolutionary in 1958. It has recently been converted into an international business centre.

La Grande Arche

Inaugurated in 1989 just in time for the bicentenary of the Revolution, La Grande Arche was the last project to be built. Designed by the Danish architect, Otto von Spreckelsen, the arch is shaped like a huge hollow cube, so vast that Notre-Dame (spire included) would fit beneath it! It is faced with glass and white Carrara marble, and is slightly out of alignment with the axis of the Voie Triomphale. The complex glass-and-steel structure of the external lifts offsets the extreme simplicity of the outline, and the *nuages* (clouds) suspended below the arch add a whimsical touch. The lifts take visitors up to the roof (le Belvédère) to admire the view.
3.5km (2¼ miles) west of the Porte Maillot. Métro & RER(A): Grande Arche de la Défense.

Malmaison

Situated 10km (6 miles) west of Paris, the elegant 17th-century Château de Malmaison is famous for its connection with Napoleon. His first wife, Joséphine de Beauharnais, bought the castle in 1799, and Napoleon always loved the place. When he divorced her in 1809 to marry Marie-Louise of Austria, Joséphine kept Malmaison for a short while until her premature death in 1814. Napoleon revisited the castle when he escaped from the island of Elba and returned to France, and again, just before he was finally exiled on the island of St Helena.

The castle had many owners before it was eventually donated to the nation

and turned into a museum, housing mementoes of Napoleon and Joséphine. Some of the original furniture from their various residences is on display.
Musée National du Château de Malmaison, avenue du Château, 92500 Rueil-Malmaison. Tel: 01 41 29 05 55. Open: weekdays 10am–5.45pm, Sat–Sun 10am–6.15pm (summer); weekdays 10am–12.30pm & 1.30–5.15pm, Sat–Sun 10am–12.30pm & 1.30–5.45pm (winter). Closed: Tue. Admission charge. RER: La Défense. Bus: 258 to Le Château.

The nearby **Château de Bois-Préau**, which also belonged to Joséphine, is devoted to mementoes of Napoleon's exile on the island of St Helena.
1 avenue de l'Impératrice Joséphine, 92500 Rueil-Malmaison. Open: 10.30am–12.30pm, 1.30–5.45pm.

Closed: Tue. The château will be closed until 2007.

Sèvres

This small town, 10km (6 miles) west of Paris, has become synonymous with beautiful china. The Manufacture Nationale de Porcelaine began making fine porcelain here in the 18th century. Its specialities include the famous *bleu de Sèvres*, a deep blue on a pure white background, and exquisite *biscuits*, unglazed delicate statuettes.

Founded in 1824, the Musée National de la Céramique contains precious exhibits from all over the world.
Place de la Manufacture, 92310 Sèvres. Tel: 01 41 14 04 20. Open: 10am–5pm. Closed: Tue. Admission charge. Métro: Pont de Sèvres.

The cavernous Grande Arche de la Défense has a rooftop exhibition gallery

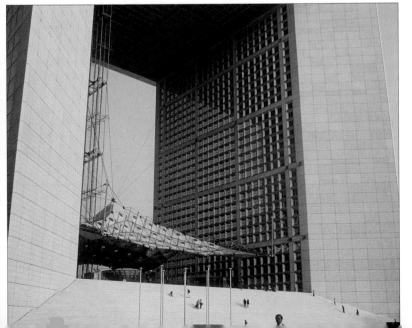

Baron Haussmann's revolution

Just over 150 years ago, a revolution shook Paris to its very foundations and altered the city more drastically than 1789 had done. It was orchestrated by one man, Baron Haussmann, with the enthusiastic approval of Napoleon III. By 1850, the town had grown round its medieval centre without any coherence, and the squalid, narrow streets were a constant health hazard. Moreover, growing social problems threatened the fragile political stability.

From 1853 to 1870, Haussmann's engineers and architects cut right through the heart of the old city, laying waste whole districts, installing an adequate water supply and a network of sewers, creating wide avenues, and building rows and rows of six-storey blocks of flats which have become one of the familiar sights of the town.

Modern Paris emerged out of the chaos and soon became known as *la ville lumière*, a harmonious ensemble of green open spaces, including the Bois de Boulogne, of spacious, tree-lined boulevards, and imposing public buildings such as the Opéra.

Haussmann's far-seeing town planning was conceived on a scale that left room for expansion, and by the end of the century the railway stations, the

Eiffel Tower, and the Grand and the Petit Palais had all taken their rightful place on the Paris scene.

The painful surgery Haussmann imposed on the capital was, however, much criticised at the time by such public figures as Victor Hugo, George Sand and Alexandre Dumas who denounced the ruthless break with the past, and the crippling cost of these 'extravagant' schemes which encouraged speculation. But history has passed a more favourable judgement, for it was Haussmann who enabled Paris to blossom into the unique capital city it is today.

Georges Eugène Haussmann, town planner extraordinaire, whose vision created modern Paris – with buildings like the Petit Palais (opposite) and the Opéra (above)

St-Denis

This industrialised and somewhat rough northern suburb is worth the visit for its beautiful Gothic cathedral, where most French monarchs have been buried.

The legend of Saint-Denis

The first bishop of Paris, Saint-Denis, martyred in Montmartre, is said to have walked, holding his head in his hands, to a field where he died and was buried. His grave soon became a place of pilgrimage, and the first church was built there in the 5th century; then, in 630, King Dagobert founded a powerful abbey to control the growing numbers of pilgrims. He was buried in the new church, which became the traditional burial place of his successors.

The Gothic church

Abbot Suger is closely linked to the history of the present cathedral. Born of poor parents, he was taken into care by the abbey. His exceptional gifts having won him the confidence of Louis VII, he became abbot of St-Denis in 1122 and designed a great Gothic cathedral which served as a prototype for later masterpieces such as Chartres Cathedral. The edifice was completed in just over ten years. During the second half of the 13th century, Saint-Louis had the nave and transept rebuilt by Pierre de Montreuil, the architect of the Ste-Chapelle, but the beautiful façade remained unaltered.

Grossly neglected over the centuries, the cathedral suffered great damage during the 1789 Revolution. Restoration work carried out in the 19th century involved the pulling down of the north tower. Viollet-le-Duc, who also restored Notre-Dame, finally undertook to save what was left.

The cathedral today

The façade looks mutilated without its north tower. The base of the towers, over the rose window, is crenellated, a reminder that the edifice was originally fortified. The tympanum of the main portal illustrates the *Last Judgement*, the other two being connected with Saint-Denis.

The cathedral is, above all, a museum of the French monarchy, with its numerous funeral monuments carved by the greatest sculptors. In the 13th century, Saint-Louis commissioned monuments for his predecessors, the most remarkable being Dagobert's imposing tomb. It became the tradition for later kings to have their own grave designed. Some, dating from the Renaissance, are particularly elaborate, such as the monument commissioned by Catherine de Médicis for herself and Henri II.

In the Romanesque crypt is the collective grave of all the Bourbons.

Bearly friends at the Bois de Vincennes

*Place de l'Hôtel de Ville, 93200
St-Denis. Tel: 01 48 09 83 54.
Open: 10am–5pm (7pm in summer).
Métro: St-Denis-Basilique.*

Vincennes

The Château and Bois de Vincennes lie just beyond the Périphérique, on the eastern side of Paris.

The Château

Situated on the edge of what was once a royal hunting ground, the Château de Vincennes dates from the 14th century. During the reign of Louis XIV, architect Le Vau built pavilions on either side of the courtyard. By then the keep had become a state prison, Fouquet and Mirabeau being among its unwilling guests. Extensive work has now restored the castle as it was in the 17th century.

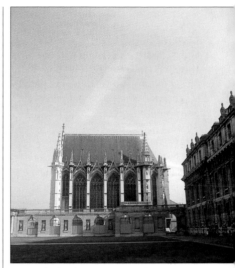

The Royal Chapel in the grounds of Vincennes

Near the entrance, the Tour du Village, which formed part of the fortified wall, is the only one to have retained its original height of 42m (138ft). The imposing keep, 52m (171ft) high, is surrounded by a separate wall and moat. It houses a museum depicting the castle's history.
*Avenue de Paris, 94300 Vincennes.
Tel: 01 43 28 15 48. Open: 10am–5pm
(6pm in summer). Closed: noon–1.15pm.
Admission charge. Métro: Château de
Vincennes.*

The Bois de Vincennes

Generations of French schoolchildren know this as the place where Saint-Louis used to administer justice seated under an oak tree. In 1860 Baron Haussmann remodelled it into an English-style park, with a racecourse. There is also the **Parc Floral de Paris** and a **zoo** here.
*Parc Floral de Paris, route de la Pyramide.
Tel: 01 55 94 20 20.
www.parcfloraldeparis.com. Open:
9.30am–5pm (8pm in summer).
Admission charge.
Métro: Château de Vincennes.
Parc zoologique – 53 avenue Daumesnil.
Open: 9am–6pm (6.30pm Sun).
Admission charge. Métro: Porte Dorée.*

Palais de la Porte Dorée

This magnificent aquarium has a large collection of tropical fish and even a pit with crocodiles. It is especially popular with children of all ages – they love the display of electric fish! Admission can be combined with Vincennes Zoo.
*293 avenue Daumesnil, 75012. Tel: 01 44
74 84 80. Open: daily except Tue,
10am–5.15pm. Admission charge.
Métro: Porte Dorée.*

Further afield

CHANTILLY

Situated north of Paris on the edge of an ancient forest, in the heart of horse-racing country, the Château de Chantilly is surrounded by a beautiful park with ponds and lakes.

The castle

The history of the castle goes back to Roman times: Cantilius was the first nobleman to build a fortified house on the site. In the 16th century the house was replaced by a castle with a splendid Renaissance edifice, and the Petit Château was built next to it. In 1662 Le Nôtre remodelled the gardens and park. One of Louis Philippe's sons, the Duc d'Aumale, rebuilt the Grand Château, damaged during the Revolution. On his death in 1897, he left the whole estate to the nation, including his magnificent art collections, which form the basis of the Condé museum.

The museum

In the Petit Château are the former private apartments. The library contains the precious 15th-century illuminated manuscript of *Les Très Riches Heures du Duc de Berry*. In the chapel there is an altar carved by Jean Goujon, and some 16th-century stained glass. In the Grand Château there are paintings by Poussin, Corot, Raphael, Watteau, Ingres and Botticelli, a unique collection of portraits by Clouet, father and son, and the famous Grand Condé diamond, which was stolen in 1926, but found later in an apple where it had been hidden by the thieves.

The park

Most of Le Nôtre's masterpiece of landscape gardening remains: the grand canal and its waterfall, and the shorter canal lined with formal gardens leading to the raised terrace. The *hameau* (hamlet), added in the 18th century, is similar to the more famous one in Versailles. The Jardin

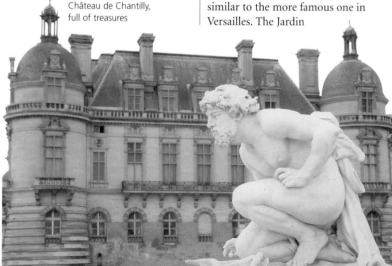

Château de Chantilly, full of treasures

Anglais (English garden) was designed in 1820.

The Grandes Ecuries

The vast stable was designed in the 18th century to house 250 horses, 500 dogs and 100 attendants. It is now a museum. *The Prix du Jockey-Club-Lancia* and the *Prix de Diane-Hermès* are run every year in June on the beautiful racecourse in front of the stables.
35km (22 miles) north of Paris.
Open: 10am–6pm. Closed: Tue.
Admission charge.

CHARTRES

Chartres is the main town of the vast plain of La Beauce, 85km (53 miles) southwest of Paris. In the centre of the old town, on the left bank of the River Eure, stands one of the most beautiful cathedrals in France. Rebuilt in the space of 25 years after a fire destroyed part of the Romanesque edifice in 1194, spared by wars and revolutions, the cathedral is a unique example of French early Gothic style showing remarkable architectural unity. Pilgrims have been flocking to Chartres since medieval times and, in 1935, students started their own pilgrimage, which takes place every year at the end of April.

The façade

The originality of the façade stems from the contrast between the sombre outline of the Clocher Vieux on the right, in pure Romanesque style, and the rich decoration of the slightly taller spire of the Clocher Neuf, added in 1506. The Portail Royal, famous for its series of tall, column-like figures, and the three

windows above it are 12th-century, the rest being 13th-century. The portals of the north and south transepts, dating from the 13th century, are equally remarkable.

The interior

The proportions are vast, with an overall length of 130m (427ft) and a height of 37m (121ft). The Gothic nave, the widest in France, appears relatively short in comparison with the transept and chancel. In the faint light, the deep, rich colours of the stained-glass windows, dating from the 12th and 13th centuries, immediately capture the attention. The elaborate choir-screen, with its 41 groups of sculptures depicting the life of Christ and the Virgin Mary, was designed in 1514 by Jehan de Beauce. The crypt is the largest in France and the oldest part of the cathedral. There are traces of a Gallo-Roman wall and a deep well.

The old town between the cathedral and the river has been renovated, and offers a pleasant journey back in time, especially along the rue des Ecuyers and adjacent streets.
Admission charge to the crypt and gallery of the Clocher Neuf.

Chartres Cathedral, a magnet for pilgrims

COURANCES

The Château de Courances lies 55km (34 miles) south of Paris in wooded country. It is near the small town of Milly-la-Forêt, famous for its beautiful 15th-century covered market.

The original Renaissance castle was remodelled in the early 17th century into a fine example of Louis XIII style. The intricate design of the brick panels, accentuated by stone borders, is offset by the absence of decoration, while the steep slate roofs add an interesting contrast of colours. The outline of the strictly symmetrical edifice is enhanced by the softness of the green setting, reflected in the water of the moat and artificial lakes. A copy of the famous staircase at Fontainebleau was added in the 19th century. The castle is still inhabited and only open at weekends.

The gardens were planned by Le Nôtre, who gave a romantic aspect to his masterly design through the use of reflection in the water of several canals supplied by the nearby River Ecole.
Guided visits on weekends 2.30–6pm, from Apr–Oct. Tel: 01 64 98 41 18. Admission charge. This visit can be combined with that of the Château de Fontainebleau, 17km (11 miles) to the east.

DAMPIERRE

About 36km (22 miles) southwest of Paris, Dampierre-en-Yvelines is a small community situated at the heart of the Parc Naturel Régional de la Haute Vallée de Chevreuse, a protected rural area. The castle stands out against the dark wooded setting of the vast park laid out by Le Nôtre.

The 16th-century castle, rebuilt in the late 17th century for Colbert's son-in-law, has been the property of the Luynes family ever since; it was restored during the first half of the 19th century. The elegant brick and stone façade is flanked by two arcaded buildings on either side.

The ground-floor reception rooms have Louis XIV and Louis XV wood panelling. On the first floor are the royal apartments, splendidly decorated to honour the monarchs who stayed at Dampierre on various occasions: Louis XIV, Louis XV and Louis XVI. At the top of the monumental staircase, the large reception room, decorated with murals by Ingres, is most remarkable. A colourful floral garden occupies part of the park.
Château de Dampierre. Tel: 01 30 52 53 24. Open: daily 2–6pm (10.30am–7pm July–Aug). Admission charge.

Handsomely proportioned Dampierre Castle

ECOUEN

Ecouen is a peaceful community in the green belt surrounding Paris. Barely 20km (12 miles) north of the city, it is famous for its Renaissance castle, which houses the Musée National de la Renaissance.

The castle was built in the early 16th century for Anne de Montmorency. Like Chantilly, Ecouen became the property of the Condé family from whom it was confiscated during the 1789 Revolution. It was later used by Napoleon as a school for the daughters of members of the Légion d'Honneur. The façade is adorned with columns and surmounted by dormer windows with carved pediments. It has recently been turned into a museum of Renaissance art to relieve the overcrowded Musée National du Moyen Age – Thermes de Cluny (*see p86*).

Furniture, wood panels, tapestries, ceramics – 8,000 exhibits in all are displayed in 34 rooms, which have retained their original decoration whenever possible, in particular their painted mantelpieces. On the ground floor there is a superb collection of arms; on the first floor, the private apartments of Montmorency and his wife have some interesting furniture, while a fine 16th-century tapestry, 75m (246ft) long, takes up the whole of one wing. On the second floor, there are numerous 16th- and 17th-century ceramic compositions, stained glass with religious motifs, painted wood panels, enamels, and so on. *Château d'Ecouen. Tel: 01 34 38 38 50. Open: daily except Tue, 9.30am–12.45pm & 2–5.15pm (5.45pm summer). Admission charge.*

Gardens at Claude Monet's house, Giverny

This visit can be combined with an excursion to the Château de Chantilly.

GIVERNY

This village, situated near the town of Vernon, 80km (50 miles) west of Paris, has strong links with Impressionism through one of the main exponents of the movement, the painter Claude Monet, who lived there from 1883 until his death in 1926. His house has been turned into a museum containing mementoes of the artist and the friends and colleagues who were his guests. The garden, which he designed himself, inspired many of his paintings, including the huge *Nymphéas* exhibited in the Musée de l'Orangerie (*see p90*). *Maison de Claude Monet. Tel: 02 32 51 28 21. Open: Apr–Oct, daily except Mon 9.30am–6pm. Admission charge.*

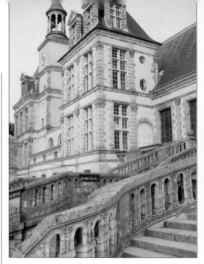

Double horseshoe staircase, Fontainebleau

FONTAINEBLEAU

Set at the heart of a splendid forest, this peaceful residential town lives in the shadow of its beautiful palace. A spring in the middle of the forest determined the choice of Fontainebleau as the site of a royal castle as far back as the 12th century. François I transformed the austere medieval castle into a magnificent Renaissance residence, sparing no expense in decorating the new buildings which form the central part of the palace. Henri IV extended the palace.

Louis XIV, Louis XV and Louis XVI contributed further to the decoration of the apartments. Spared by the Revolution, the palace continued to be used by kings and emperors until the end of the 19th century, when it was turned into a museum.

The exterior

The buildings surround four courtyards. Access to the palace is through the main courtyard, or Cour du Cheval Blanc. At the end of the courtyard is the famous 'horseshoe' staircase, from which Napoleon made a very emotional farewell to his imperial guard before his departure to Elba in 1814. Beyond is the Cour de la Fontaine, backed by the Galerie François I. The Cour de la Fontaine overlooks the Etang des Carpes, a small carp pond with a charming pavilion in its centre. Le Nôtre's formal garden is on one side of the pond, and the Jardin Anglais (English-style garden) is on the other side. In the centre of the latter is the Fontaine Bliaud. The oldest part of the palace surrounds the Cour Ovale. A monumental entrance gives access to the Cour des Offices which is lined with outbuildings dating from 1609.

The interior

The Grands Appartements (state apartments) on the first floor start with the Galerie François I, with its original Renaissance decoration of stucco and frescoes. The Escalier du Roi leads to the magnificent Salle de Bal (ballroom); the ceiling and chimney piece are particularly remarkable. On the other side of the Cour Ovale are the Appartements Royaux, the monarchs' private and official apartments, which include the Salon du Donjon, the only remaining part of the medieval castle, and the Salle du Trône, formerly the king's bedroom. In the emperor's official apartments is the famous Salon Rouge, where he abdicated in 1814.

The Petits Appartements, which are on the ground floor, were formerly the private apartments of Napoleon and Joséphine, and contain some splendid Empire furniture.

65km (40 miles) southeast of Paris.
Entrance: place du Général de Gaulle.
Tel: 01 60 71 50 70. Open: 9.30am–5pm
(6pm in summer). Closed: Tue.
Admission charge.

ROYAUMONT

The Cistercian abbey of Royaumont,
founded by Saint-Louis in 1228 and
richly endowed by his successors,
remained powerful until the Revolution.
The church was then demolished, and
the extensive abbey buildings turned
into a cotton mill. Royaumont, now
owned by a foundation, is the scene of
regular cultural activities.

Very little remains of the church.
Next to it, the cloister, which encloses a
garden, is the largest of any Cistercian
abbey in France. The long refectory,
where Saint-Louis served the monks
himself during his visits to the abbey, is a
masterpiece of early Gothic architecture.
In the kitchens, the impressive vaulted
ceiling rests on massive columns with
fine carved capitals.

30km (19 miles) north of
Paris. Tel: 01 30 35 59 00.

Open: daily 10am–6pm. Admission
charge. This excursion can be combined
with a trip to Chantilly.

ST-GERMAIN-EN-LAYE

This important residential town, 18km
(11 miles) west of Paris, has a history
going back to the building of the first
castle in the 12th century. The
Renaissance castle, erected in 1539 by
Pierre Chambiges on the same site, was
later extended by Jules Hardouin-
Mansart, and the park and gardens were
designed by Le Nôtre, including a
magnificent Grande Terrasse, 2.4km
($1^1/2$ miles) long.

In 1855, Napoleon III restored the
castle to its original state and set up the
Musée des Antiquités Nationales. The
museum's archaeological collections
cover France's past from the palaeolithic
period to the Dark Ages, and include a
reconstruction of the famous Salle des
Taureaux at Lascaux.
Place du Château. Tel: 01 39 10 13 00.
Museum open: 9am–5.15pm.
Closed: Tue. Admission charge. RER:
St-Germain-en-Laye.

Castle museum of
St-Germain-en-Laye

THEME PARKS

This popular form of family entertainment is represented in the Paris region by Disneyland® Paris, situated some 35km (22 miles) east of the capital in the countryside of Marne-la-Vallée, France Miniature (25km/16 miles west) and the Parc Astérix (25km/16 miles north).

Disneyland® Paris

At the heart of Disneyland® Resort Paris is the theme Disneyland® Park – only part of a vast holiday resort covering nearly 2,000 ha (4,942 acres), one-fifth the size of Paris. Next to Disneyland® Park is the newly opened Walt Disney Studios® Park, a behind-the-scenes world of film, television and animation where you can see some of your favourite characters.

Disneyland® Park, with its five magical lands, is an amazing mixture of fantasy and adventure where you can meet Mickey Mouse, fly with Dumbo, explore the Swiss Family Robinson's tree house, be propelled to the moon through Space Mountain, and return to ground to follow the tracks of Indiana Jones™ and the Temple of Peril: Backwards. The resort also has seven themed hotels, a golf course and Disney® Village, which offers a whole range of restaurants and shops and plenty of entertainment for both day and night.

Marne-la-Vallée, 77700. Tel: 08 25 30 60 30. www.disneylandparis.com.
Open: all year; daily timings vary with the seasons. Admission charge.
RER: Chessy (end of the line).

France Miniature

This theme park will take you on a lightning journey across France, travelling from one region to the next in a few minutes. Two thousand models reduced 30 times, including 168 monuments, 20 typical villages, landscapes and scenes of daily life, are spread over a vast relief map of France that covers 5 ha (12 acres).

There are shops selling crafts and other products from the regions of France, exhibitions, stands where you can sample regional cuisine, a picnic area and two restaurants.

Parc Astérix

25 route du Mesnil, Elancourt. Tel: 01 30 16 16 30. www.franceminiature.com. Open: 10am–6pm (until 7pm July–Aug). Closed: Nov–Mar and certain days at other times, so check first. Admission charge. RER: St-Quentin-en-Yvelines, then shuttle service to the theme park.

Parc Astérix
The setting is France under Roman occupation 2,000 years ago, seen through the eyes of the characters created by Albert Uderzo for his series of *Astérix* comic strips, in which the intelligent and cunning Gauls constantly outwit the dumb Romans.

Astérix, the hero, is the brain behind the action, and Obelix, his fat devoted friend, lends him his muscle power, with Getafix the druid and many others. But there is more. Parc Astérix is an adventure park with many outdoor activities for the whole family; shops in Via Antiqua and rue de Paris, a medieval square with its crowd of jugglers and acrobats, and two restaurants.
60128 Plailly. Tel: 08 92 68 30 10. Open: Apr–Oct 10am–6pm (July, Aug & weekends 9.30am–7pm). Admission charge. RER: Roissy, then shuttle service to the park.

VAUX-LE-VICOMTE
Situated 51km (32 miles) southeast of Paris, the Château de Vaux-le-Vicomte is a masterpiece of 17th-century French architecture. Fouquet, Louis XIV's finance minister, had gathered a colossal fortune and decided to build a castle that would be a symbol of his success. In 1656 he commissioned the best artists of his time, and no expense was spared. An army of 18,000 workers slaved away at the construction of the castle which was completed in just five years, and Fouquet invited Louis XIV to a splendid reception that greatly surpassed those given at court. Dishes of solid gold crowned dozens of buffet tables set out in the garden, while jewel-studded elephants lined the alleys of orange trees, and Chinese fireworks were shot off from the ponds. The king was so annoyed that he had Fouquet – who had already fallen from favour – arrested a few days later. After a lengthy trial the ambitious minister was condemned to life imprisonment. The castle changed hands several times during the next 200 years until it was bought by a rich industrialist, whose family have since restored both house and gardens.

The main building stands on a raised terrace surrounded by a moat. On the ground floor, six reception rooms on either side of the oval Grand Salon (drawing room) overlook the magnificent gardens. The frescoes on the ceilings, depicting mythological scenes, are by Le Brun. A staircase in the entrance hall gives access to the first-floor private apartments. From the terrace, the view sweeps across the gardens, which extend a long way on different levels, and are adorned with ornamental ponds, cascades and a Grand Canal. In the stables there is a museum of horse-drawn carriages.
Vaux-le-Vicomte, 77950 Maincy, near Melun. Tel: 01 64 14 41 90. Open: end Mar to mid-Nov 10am–6pm. Admission charge. Saturday candlelit visits from May–Sept 8pm–midnight. Cafeteria. RER: Melun, then by taxi for 6km (3¾ miles).

Versailles

For most people, Versailles is the supreme example of an aspect of French culture that blends elegance and refinement with a search for perfection, and that is sometimes coupled with excessive formality and bold confidence.

One of the château's exquisite ceilings

A most ambitious project

In 1661, Louis XIV, the Sun King, decided to build a castle that would outshine Vaux-le-Vicomte (*see p131*) on the site of the modest brick-and-stone château built by Philibert Le Roy for his father in 1631.

For nearly 50 years the greatest artists worked at Versailles: the architect Le Vau, succeeded by Hardouin-Mansart; Le Brun, who supervised the interior decoration; and Le Nôtre, who surpassed himself in the design of the magnificent gardens. The King and his court moved in during 1682 – a total of 3,000 people, attending sumptuous receptions. From 1682 to 1789, Versailles was also the political centre of France.

During the Revolution, the furniture was sold, and the château gradually fell into disrepair until, in 1837, Louis-Philippe had it converted into a museum of French history.

After World War I, total restoration of the castle was undertaken with the financial help of US philanthropist J D Rockefeller, and Versailles has slowly regained its 18th-century elegance.

The château

The approach to the château, one of the most visited monuments in France, is very impressive. There is a succession of three open courtyards to be traversed, the Court of Ministers, the Royal Court and the Court of Marble, and Louis XIV's statue in the centre.

On the garden side, the 680-m (2,231-ft) long façade has a projecting central section. An elegant balustrade emphasises the roof line, and groups of elegant columns at regular intervals attract the eye as focal points.

State Apartments

On the way to the State Apartments, look at the chapel. This was designed by Hardouin-Mansart but only completed after his death in 1710.

The State Apartments include a suite of reception rooms, decorated with marble and paintings; they were used for the entertainment of the court during the winter season.

The large windows of the 75-m (246-ft) long Galerie des Glaces (Hall of Mirrors), the most famous room in the palace, which overlooks the gardens, let in the setting sun. This reflects on the huge mirrors (which do not retain the original glass) covering the walls.

Next come the Queen's Apartments, in particular the Queen's bedroom where Louis XV and many royal children were born. The King's Apartments are in Louis XIII's castle. The bedroom, remodelled by Louis XIV, was used by his successors until 1789. Next door is the Chambre du Conseil (Council Chamber).

Château de Versailles, place d'Armes. Tel: 01 30 97 89 89. Open: daily except Mon. Admission charge. Free parking. RER: Versailles-Rive gauche. Château open: 9am–5.30pm (6.30pm in summer). Park open: 7am–dusk summer, 8am– dusk winter.

Visits – without guide: Chapel & State Apartments: from entrance A on the right. With guide: Appartement du Roi, last visit starts at 4pm. Appartements du Dauphin et de la Dauphine et de Mesdames: guided visits during daylight hours.

Events: Every Sat & Sun Apr–Sept, there is a spectacular fountain show, with music, 11am–noon, 3.30–5pm. Combined fountains and firework displays are also held on some Saturday nights in summer.

Versailles

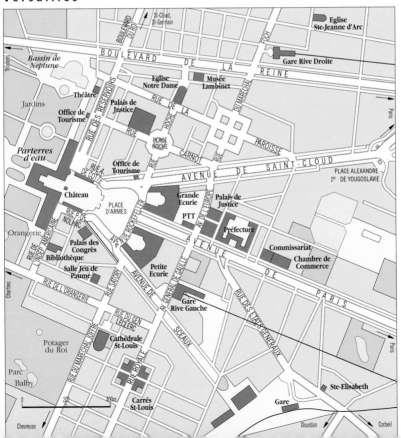

Cabinets Intérieurs du Roi

The King's private apartments, designed by Gabriel for Louis XV, include the bedroom where the King died in 1774, the games room, the study with its original desk, the music room, which Louis XV furnished for his favourite daughter, Madame Adélaïde, and where the young Wolfgang Mozart is supposed to have played in 1763, and the beautiful library.

The **Cabinets Intérieurs de la Reine** were private apartments originally designed for Louis XV's queen, and were later refurbished for Marie Antoinette.

Opéra Royal

Built by Gabriel, the opera house was inaugurated in 1770 for the wedding of Marie Antoinette to the future Louis XVI. It could seat 700 spectators and

Versailles – Le Parc

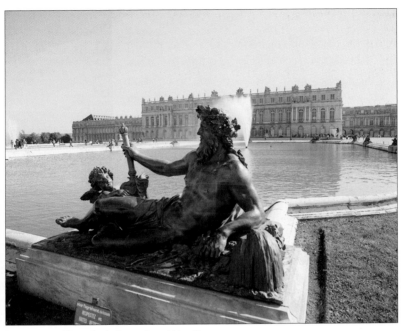

Waterways and fountains in the gardens at Versailles

could also be used as a grand reception room or a ballroom. On the ground floor are the recently renovated Appartements du Dauphin et de la Dauphine (the heirs to the throne), and those of Louis XV's daughters.

The gardens

From the raised terrace in front of the château, the Grand Canal offers a magnificent vista which extends to the woods in the distance. The design of the gardens by Le Nôtre, between 1661 and 1668, is a masterpiece of geometry: the canal is the focal point of a composition on different levels, of ornamental ponds adorned with fountains, flowerbeds, bowers and over 200 sculptures.

The Trianons

The Trianons are lesser palaces. The Grand Trianon, faced with pink marble, was built by Hardouin-Mansart for Louis XIV, who wished to give private receptions for Madame de Maintenon.

The Petit Trianon was commissioned by Louis XV and given by Louis XVI to Marie Antoinette, who used it to be alone with her children. She had the garden completely remodelled and the charming *hameau* (hamlet) built nearby. *Cabinets Intérieurs de la Reine: guided tours: 9am–5pm (6pm in summer). Opéra Royal: last guided visit starts 4pm. Grand and Petit Trianons open: as for château, 9am–5.30pm (6.30pm in summer). Entrance A on the right.*

Gardens and greenery

A large city can become oppressive after a while, and you may suddenly feel the need to get away from the crowds and the incessant noise, particularly with the arrival of warm, sunny weather in late spring or summer. Paris and the Ile-de-France offer plenty of opportunities for a change of pace and scenery, in parks and floral gardens, in forests teeming with wildlife, and along quiet rivers.

The Bois: a slice of the countryside in the city

Bois de Boulogne

This favourite haunt of nature-loving Parisians, covering about 850 ha (2,100 acres), is crowded at weekends, but offers peace and quiet to those who wander off the beaten track along its shady avenues (take care after dusk). Many family activities are available: boating on the lakes, cycling along specially designed lanes, horse riding and fishing. The **Jardin d'Acclimatation**, on the northern edge of the 'Bois', is a comprehensive amusement park for children with rides, a train and a zoo; and there are clearly marked picnic areas.

This former royal hunting forest used to abound with deer, bear and wild boar until Louis XV opened it to the public and it became fashionable. Given to the city of Paris in 1852 by Napoleon III, it was remodelled into an English-style park by Baron Haussmann, who created lakes, ponds and the Longchamp racecourse. The Auteuil racecourse was built after the Franco-Prussian War in 1870, and at the turn of the 20th century fashionable horse-drawn carriages could be seen driving along the wide avenues that nowadays carry fast traffic bound for the *banlieue* (suburbs) just across the Seine.

In the northwest corner of the 'Bois' is the **Parc de Bagatelle**, a beautiful garden well known for its spring display of tulips and irises, and roses and water lilies in summer. The nearby **Jardins de Bagatelle** is an expensive restaurant in a lovely setting.

The **Pré Catelan**, in the centre of the Bois de Boulogne, is another attractive park with a magnificent 200-year-old copper beech; next to it, the **Jardin Shakespeare**, planted with flowers and trees mentioned in Shakespeare's plays, has a charming open-air theatre.
Entry from the north side. Métro: Les Sablons, Porte Maillot. Bagatelle, métro: Pont-de-Neuilly then No 43 bus to place de Bagatelle. East side, RER: Avenue-Henri-Martin. South side, métro: Porte d'Auteuil. Bicycle rental available at the lakes; horse riding at the Centre Hippique, route de la Muette à Neuilly. Tel: 01 45 01 20 06.

Bois de Vincennes

See p123.

Jardin Albert-Khan

Situated just south of the Bois de Boulogne, this succession of gardens, created by the banker Albert-Khan, illustrates landscapes from different regions of the world: the forest of Vosges, a Japanese garden, an English garden, as well as a picturesque rock setting. The display of hundreds of flowers is at its best in late spring.

14 rue du Port, 92100 Boulogne. Open: 11am–6pm. Admission charge. Métro: Pont-de-St-Cloud, then bus No 72, 52 or 175.

Jardin des Serres d'Auteuil

Plants used for decorating public buildings and for official occasions are grown in the greenhouses surrounding this municipal garden.

The huge tropical house contains palm trees, banana trees and a host of tropical plants. Rare species are housed in a number of hothouses on the south side of the garden.

3 avenue de la Porte d'Auteuil, 75016. Open: daily 10am–5pm (6pm in summer). Admission charge. Métro: Porte d'Auteuil.

Orangerie, Parc de Bagatelle, the 'Bois'

The role of the river

Rising in the Langres plateau just northwest of Dijon and discharging into the English Channel, the Seine has played a vital role in the birth and development of the city of Paris.

The first settlers to occupy the area were fishermen, and for hundreds of years the river provided food, water and protection to the people who lived on the Ile-de-la-Cité. When commerce became essential to the survival of the rapidly developing city, the Seine (the third-longest river in France) was the obvious means of communication, and proved quite lucrative for those who levied substantial tolls.

Because the economy of Paris depended on the river, it was natural that those who sought to rule the city should also seek to control its main port which, in medieval times, was La Grève (now the place de l'Hôtel de Ville). In the 13th century, the guild of merchants obtained from the king the right to levy taxes from ships bringing in essential goods such as salt, wine and wood. The harbour developed rapidly, and today Paris is the main river port, and the fourth most important harbour in France.

The Seine has contributed much to their prosperity, and Parisians really love their river. They have built their most prestigious monuments along its banks, adorned it with beautiful bridges, and lined its embankment with trees to provide shade so that they can stroll

there after a day's work or sit on one of the benches and relax in the evening.

The river's sometimes erratic behaviour can now be controlled, but memorable floods have been recorded in the past. Even today, whenever the river rises above its normal level, people flock eagerly to the Pont de l'Alma to see how much of the famous Zouave is under water.

Facing page: Zouave keeps a watchful eye on the water level at Pont de l'Alma; below: excursions on the Bateaux Mouches

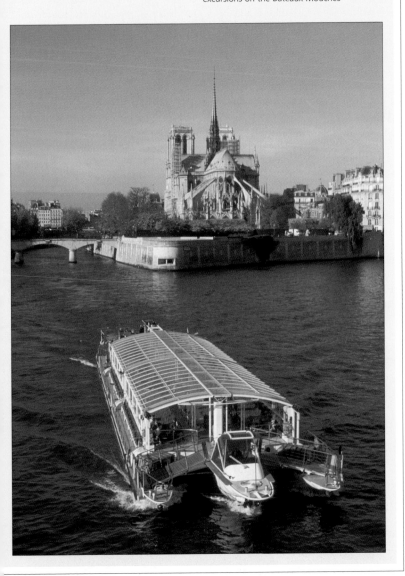

Jardin des Plantes

Founded in 1626, the botanical gardens were greatly extended by the famous 18th-century naturalist, Buffon, and the menagerie was created during the Revolution. The Musée d'Histoire Naturelle (Museum of Natural History) houses departments of botany, mineralogy, palaeontology and entomology. The gardens include the Jardin Alpin with 2,000 species of plants from mountainous regions from the Alps to the Himalayas; the Jardin d'Hiver housing heavy-scented tropical plants and flowers; a number of hothouses; a maze; and a herb garden devoted to medicinal plants.

Entrance from rue Cuvier, rue Buffon and Place Valhubert, 75005.
Tel: 01 40 79 30 00. Gardens, menagerie, museum and maze open daily 7.30am–5.30pm (8pm in summer).
Free admission.
Métro: Jussieu, Gare d'Austerlitz.

Parc des Buttes-Chaumont

Situated in the 19th *arrondissement*, east of the centre, this park was landscaped by Haussmann on hilly wasteland. From the small temple, romantically set on the island in the middle of the lake, the view extends to the Butte Montmartre.
Métro: Buttes-Chaumont.

Parc Georges Brassens

Two bronze bulls at the main entrance are a reminder that the park was created on the site of the former Vaugirard slaughterhouses. A small garden filled with scented plants was specially designed for blind people, and the vineyard is the scene of festivities during the grape harvest in October.
Rue des Morillons, 75015.
Métro: Convention.

Parc Monceau

Situated in a fashionable residential area, close to the Arc de Triomphe, the

The delightfully landscaped Parc Monceau

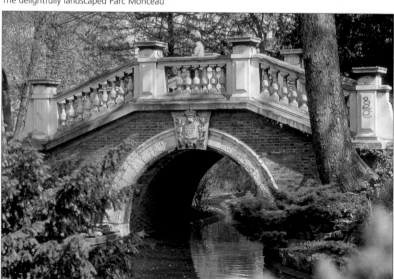

Parc Monceau was landscaped as an English garden, with rocks and an oddly shaped lake, and adorned with mock ruins, pyramids and statues following the neoclassical style fashionable in the 18th century.
Boulevard de Courcelles.
Métro: Monceau.

Parc Montsouris

Another of Haussmann's creations, this hilly park facing the Cité Universitaire (the student halls of residence) includes a large lake, waterfalls, a meteorological observatory and a reproduction of the Bardo, the Bey of Tunis' palace.
Boulevard Jourdan.
RER: Cité-Universitaire.

Parc de St-Cloud

Situated in one of the elegant western suburbs overlooking the Seine, this park was designed by Le Nôtre. The castle, where Napoleon stayed many times, was destroyed by fire in 1870. The Grande Cascade, with its statues featuring the Seine and the Marne rivers, is particularly remarkable; so is the view across Paris from the terrace. The woods in the upper part of the park offer lovely cool walks in summer.
On the N186, 11km (6.8 miles) west of Paris.

OUT OF TOWN

The green belt round Paris includes several woodland areas, the largest being the Forêt de Rambouillet and the Forêt de Fontainebleau. There are also many rivers that wind their way towards the Seine along picturesque valleys such as the Vallée de Chevreuse with its quiet, twisting roads. The ideal means to achieve complete relaxation is to join a leisurely cruise along the Seine for a few hours, or even a whole day.

Forêt de Fontainebleau

This vast forest surrounding the castle and town of Fontainebleau over an area of 25,000 ha (61,774 acres) offers a landscape of wooded hills and valleys, of moors covered with heather and gorse, and of large rocks piled high in places. Pines, oaks and beeches make up the majority of the forest. There are opportunities for rock climbing, and the area has become popular with amateurs and professionals.

Various itineraries are suggested in the *Guide des sentiers de promenades dans le Massif forestier de Fontainebleau*, available from the tourist office in Fontainebleau. Most tours start from the town. To the west are the Gorges de Franchard, a narrow glen scattered with impressive overhanging rocks. To the south, Le Long Rocher is a rock-strewn plateau that affords lovely views over the forest.
60km (37 miles) southeast of Paris.

Spend the day in Fontainebleau forest

Forêt de Rambouillet

Although less spectacular than Fontainebleau, this forest, covering 20,000 ha (49,419 acres), offers pleasant walks and cycle tours through ancient villages, along narrow rivers and beside picturesque lakes. Oak and pine predominate, and red deer and wild boar are plentiful, if not always easy to detect.

In the isolated northern part of the forest, fishermen seek peace and quiet on the shores of the Etang Neuf, near the solitary 16th-century castle of La Mormaire and the almost deserted village of Gambaiseuil. Further south, from the Rochers d'Angennes, a rock formation on high ground, there is a good view of the Etang d'Angennes, overgrown with reeds, and the secluded valley of the Guesle River.

L'Haÿ-les-Roses

Situated in the densely populated southern suburbs, halfway between Paris and Orly Airport, the rose garden of l'Haÿ-les-Roses was created 100 years ago; thousands of roses, wild, as well as hybrids, offer a grand display of colours in a charming setting framed with climbers. There is also a Musée de la Rose devoted to works of art connected with this aristocratic flower: prints, embroidery, ceramics and small objets d'art.

8km (5 miles) south of Paris.

Parc de Sceaux

The gardens were designed by Le Nôtre, and Louis XIV was invited to a splendid reception to mark the inauguration of the castle, built in 1670. During the Revolution, the estate was bought for the use of the land and the castle was demolished. The state acquired the property in 1923, and undertook its restoration.

Once more, water is the focal point of the beautiful gardens: on the south side, a wide avenue leads to the Grandes Cascades, a succession of waterfalls supplying an octagonal lake surrounded by plane trees reflected in the still water; the grand canal is also lined with trees, which create contrasts of sunlight and shade, and temper the formal aspect of French-style gardens.

The Petit Château and the Pavillon de l'Aurore (in the northeast corner of the

WILDLIFE

You do not have to be a connoisseur to appreciate the subtle blend of colours and the fresh scent of woodland flowers in springtime. In the verdant Forêt de Fontainebleau, hyacinths, daffodils and laburnum herald the return of warm weather, followed by hawthorn blossoms and fragile lilies-of-the-valley. Later on, dense bushes of gorse light up the green undergrowth, eclipsing the more discreet heather, campanulas and wild carnations. Summer offers the pleasure of looking for wild strawberries and raspberries, while autumn brings hazelnuts and chestnuts. These traditional hunting grounds still abound with roe deer and boar, as well as the more common foxes, hare and squirrels. There is also a great variety of birdlife, including the famous Fontainebleau woodpeckers.

park) date from the 17th century. In the latter there is an audiovisual presentation of the estate.
10km (6 miles) southwest of Paris.

Vallée de Chevreuse

The upper valley of the River Yvette is known as the Vallée de Chevreuse after the small town dominated by the ruins of its castle. In 1984, a regional park was created to preserve this area of natural beauty, consisting of woodland, lush meadows and cultivated land. The D58, which follows the river westwards, leads to the Château de Dampierre (*see p126*). To the north are the ruins of the Cistercian abbey of Port-Royal-des-Champs, famous in the 17th century for its criticism of the Jesuits. The southern road (D24) leads to Les Vaux de Cernay, where a picturesque stream makes its way through woods and rocks.
The town of Chevreuse is situated 30km (19 miles) southwest of Paris.

Walk or cycle in the Forêt de Rambouillet

Shopping

Part of the fun of staying in Paris is the opportunity to go on a shopping spree. Deciding where to go, however, can be quite bewildering in any large city, and particularly in Paris, where attractive shop windows are to be found round every street corner.

Paris is famous for its designer outlets

Before you embark on a shopping tour of Paris there are a few facts you should be aware of.

It is dangerous to carry large amounts of cash, as pickpockets frequent crowded places. The safest and most widely used method of payment in boutiques, department stores and shopping centres is by credit card; but bear in mind that a minimum purchase of 15 euros is required. Be prepared to pay cash at market stalls and food kiosks.

Tax-free shopping is now common practice for non-EU residents. Look out for the symbol on shop windows. You need to spend a minimum of 183 euros to qualify for a tax refund. You will then be given a special bill in two parts; the shopkeeper will tell you where to send one of the copies for a VAT refund once it has been stamped by Customs.

Although shops remain open quite late in the evening (*see p185*), individual

For haute couture head for avenue Montaigne and rue François I

shops are often closed on Monday morning, sometimes all day Monday. So, if planning a long weekend in Paris, it is better to opt for Friday rather than Monday.

Department stores

All the large department stores except one are situated on the Right Bank. Moreover, Parisians often refer to the St-Lazare-Opéra district as the quartier des *grands magasins*, as the most prestigious of them are lined up along the boulevard Haussmann.

The **Galeries Lafayette** (*40 boulevard Haussmann, 75009, tel: 01 42 82 34 56, métro: Chaussée d'Antin*) and **Le Printemps** (*64 boulevard Haussmann, tel: 01 42 82 50 00, métro: Havre-Caumartin*), both established in the late 19th century, tend to lay emphasis more and more on elegance and fashion trends in clothes and accessories, as well as household goods. Their extensive ready-to-wear departments have attracted all the main designers. Le Printemps has devoted a separate building to menswear (Brummell).

Two other department stores situated between the Louvre and the Hôtel de Ville, along the rue de Rivoli, are less fashion-conscious and mainly sought-after for their household goods. **The Bazar de l'Hôtel de Ville**, known as the BHV (*52 rue de Rivoli, 75004, tel: 01 42 74 90 00, métro: Hôtel de Ville*), has an incredibly well-stocked DIY department in the basement. Nearby, **La Samaritaine** (*19 rue de la Monnaie, 75001, tel: 01 40 41 22 54, métro: Pont-Neuf*) attracts a similar clientele, and you can enjoy a cup of tea on the roof

Galeries Lafayette: shop till you drop

terrace while admiring the splendid view over Paris.

Le Bon Marché (*22 rue de Sèvres, 75007, tel: 01 44 39 80 00, métro: Sèvres-Babylone*) is the only department store on the Left Bank. It is rightly famous for its fine food section, **l'Epicerie**, which is open longer hours than the store itself.

Arcades

Quaint, old-fashioned and full of atmosphere, some of these arcades make a change from traditional shopping (*see pp112–13*).

Open-air markets

These are the most ancient type of markets, but they have, for some time, been in fierce competition with the large supermarkets to supply Parisian households with fresh food. However, this is one battle the big stores are not about to win, for not only do open-air markets offer their demanding customers good quality and low prices, but they are also the very fibre of a district's social life – a meeting place where neighbours of different backgrounds exchange opinions.

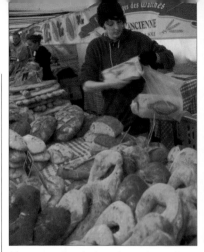

Always appealing, fresh produce at keen prices in a Montparnasse street market

Some of these markets are organised by the municipality, and usually take place on two or three mornings a week on a square or large open space. Canopied stalls are put up the night before, and early in the morning stallholders park their vans all around, usually creating huge traffic jams. They come straight from the central food market at Rungis, and their prices are generally very competitive. Two such markets can be found in the Latin Quarter – on the place Monge (*métro: Monge*) and the place Maubert (*métro: Maubert-Mutualité*).

Street markets usually run on a slightly different principle. Shops that sell fresh food in a particular street set up stands outside their premises on every day of the week except one, and advertise special offers. These markets are open until early evening to enable working people to get their daily supply of fresh vegetables on their way home. The rue Mouffetard (*métro: Censier-Daubenton*) and the rue de Buci (*métro: Mabillon*) markets in the Latin Quarter are among the best in Paris; the rue Lepic in Montmartre (*métro: Blanche*) is also very attractive and lively.

Covered markets

Steeped in tradition, these are the direct descendants of medieval structures known as *halles*, which usually consisted of a solid roof resting on large wooden pillars. Today, they are housed in proper buildings belonging to the municipality. They have cubicles all round, and fixed stalls in the centre where carefully selected shopkeepers offer good service in a friendly atmosphere. There are 13 covered markets in Paris, all to be found on the Right Bank, except one, which is situated in the rue Mabillon in St-Germain-des-Prés (*métro: Mabillon*). Another interesting market is in the rue Lebon, near the place des Ternes, in the 17th *arrondissement* (*métro: Ternes*).

Specialised markets

The loveliest flower market in Paris is situated on the place Louis-Lépine, on the northern side of the Ile-de-la-Cité (*métro: Cité*) every day from 8am to

7pm, except on Sunday when it is replaced by a bird market. Another is held on the place de la Madeleine (*métro: Madeleine*). There is also a small pet market along the quai de la Mégisserie on the Right Bank (*métro: Châtelet or Pont-Neuf*).

On the corner of the avenue de Marigny and the avenue Gabriel (*métro: Champs-Elysées-Clémenceau*), an extensive stamp market takes place on Thursday, Saturday and Sunday.

Cheap new and second-hand clothes are sold in a covered market every morning except Monday on the Carreau du Temple (*métro: Temple*).

Flea markets
The most famous flea market in Paris is the Marchés aux Puces of the Porte de Clignancourt, in St-Ouen, which takes place on Saturday, Sunday and Monday between 7.30am and 7pm, though bargains are very rare these days. Other, similar but more genuine, markets are held in the open, on Saturday and Sunday along the avenues Georges-Lafenestre and Marc-Sangnier (*métro: Porte de Vanves*), and avenue de la Porte de Montreuil (*métro: Porte de Montreuil*).

Shopping centres
In some places a wide variety of boutiques are gathered under one roof for convenience.

The Forum des Halles, rue Pierre Lescot (*métro: Les Halles, see pp54–5*), is an underground complex with shops of all sizes selling just about everything from *foie gras* to shoes. The Galeries des Champs Elysées, on the north side of the famous avenue between the Rond-

Point and the rue de Berri (*métro: Franklin-Roosevelt*), are worth exploring for their elegant boutiques, as is the vast shopping complex at La Défense, Les Quatre-Temps, which has a network of lanes lined with shops on several levels, and a huge hypermarket called **Auchan**.

Specialised streets and areas
In the 9th *arrondissement* there are busy shopping streets north of the boulevard Haussmann, with a number of stamp collectors, high-class confectioners, upmarket decorators and fashion boutiques. Not far from there, in the 8th *arrondissement*, the area round the place de l'Europe is well known for its musical-instrument makers and dealers.

On the place de la Madeleine can be found the finest high-class grocers and delicatessens in Paris: **Fauchon** and **Hédiard**.

South of the boulevard Haussmann, the avenue Matignon and rue du Faubourg St-Honoré are famous for their art galleries, while the avenue Montaigne and rue François I are the headquarters of fashion designers; the rue de la Paix and place Vendôme are

Assessing a find in the stamp market

lined with exclusive jewellers. The main glass and china manufacturers have their showrooms along the rue de Paradis, near the Gare de l'Est in the 10th *arrondissement*.

Trade exhibitions

The Chambre de Commerce et d'Industrie de Paris (*tel: 01 55 65 55 65*) and Foires Salons et Congrès de France (*tel: 01 53 90 20 00*) publish a comprehensive list of trade exhibitions in Paris. The following is a selection.

Brocante de Paris: antiques fair in early February at the *Espace Champerret, Porte de Champerret, 75017. Métro: Louise-Michel.*

Foire à la Ferraille de Paris: literally a 'scrap-iron fair', in fact an antiques fair held in February, May and September in the *Parc Floral de Paris, Bois de Vincennes, 75012. Métro: Château de Vincennes.*

Musicora: this international exhibition of classical music is held during April in the *Grand Palais, avenue Winston Churchill, 75008. Métro: Champs-Elysées-Clémenceau.*

Foire Internationale de Paris: includes tourism, books, gardens, wines, sports and entertainment; held in May at the *Parc des Expositions de Paris, Porte de Versailles, 75015. Métro: Porte de Versailles.*

Mondial de l'Automobile: motor car show held every other even year in October at the Parc des Expositions de Paris.

Salon du Cheval et du Poney: all about horses, with various activities and show jumping, held in December at the Parc des Expositions de Paris.

Antiques – worth a glance, browse or buy

Salon Nautique International: popular boat show, held just before Christmas at the Parc des Expositions de Paris.

Where to shop
Antiques
Le Louvre des Antiquaires

250 shops offer plenty of choice from French furniture to jewellery.
2 place du Palais-Royal, opposite the Louvre. Tel: 01 42 97 27 27. Métro: Palais-Royal.

Carré Rive Gauche

Next to the Musée d'Orsay; formed by the Quai Voltaire, rue des St-Pères, rue de l'Université and rue du Bac. Métro: rue du Bac.

The Village Suisse

More than 100 dealers sell good-quality ornaments and furniture.
78 avenue de Suffren. Tel: 01 43 06 69 90. Métro: La Motte-Picquet-Grenelle.

Drouot

Famous auctioneers. Salerooms at:
9 rue Drouot. Tel: 01 48 00 20 20. Métro: Richelieu-Drouot & Le Petetier. 15 avenue Montaigne. Tel: 01 48 00 20 80. Métro: Alma-Marceau.

More than 50 antique dealers are established in the tiny pedestrian streets of the **Village St-Paul** in the Marais, (*métro: St-Paul or Pont-Marie*). You can buy old prints and postcards from the booksellers on the quais along the Seine.

Books

The largest bookshops in Paris are the book departments of the **FNAC** stores in *boulevard St-Germain, Forum des Halles* and *avenue des Ternes.* The 6th *arrondissement*, in and around the boulevard St-Germain, has many traditional bookshops.

Books in English are available from:

WHSmith
248 rue de Rivoli. Tel: 01 44 77 88 99. Métro: Concorde.

Galignani
A well-stocked, old-fashioned bookshop, with bilingual service.
224 rue de Rivoli. Tel: 01 42 60 76 07. Métro: Concorde.

Brentano's
37 avenue de l'Opéra. Tel: 01 42 61 52 50. Métro: Opéra.

San Francisco Book Co.
17 rue Monsieur-le-Prince. Tel: 01 43 29 15 70. Métro: Odéon. RER: Luxembourg.

Clothes

Apart from the exclusive fashion designers in the 8th *arrondissement*, there are trendy fashion boutiques in the area round the church of St-Germain-des-Prés, while department stores have a choice of more traditional wear. Bargains can be found in the avenue de Clichy in the 17th *arrondissement.*

Gifts

Replicas from museum exhibits and objects by famous manufacturers are sold in four boutiques of the Association Paris-Musées:

Carnavalet
23 rue de Sévigné, 75003. Métro: St-Paul.

Forum des Halles
Rue Pierre Lescot. Métro: Les Halles.

Le Louvre
Métro: Palais-Royal.

Galliéra
10 avenue Pierre I de Serbie, 75016. Métro: Iéna.
*(See also **Les Bouquinistes**, p100.)*

Music

Three superstores compete to offer the best prices and a vast choice:

FNAC
Forum des Halles, 1 rue Pierre Lescot. Tel: 01 40 41 40 00. Métro: Les Halles, RER: Châtelet-les-Halles.

FNAC Etoile
26 avenue des Ternes. Tel: 01 44 09 18 00. Métro: Ternes.

Virgin Megastore
52–60 avenue des Champs-Elysées. Tel: 01 49 53 50 00. Métro: Franklin-Roosevelt.

Jewellery

Look for fashion jewellery in **Le Printemps**, the **Galeries Lafayette** (*see p145*) and the **Galerie Vivienne** (*see p97*). The top jewellers – **Boucheron**, **Cartier**, **Van Cleef & Arpels** – are in the place Vendôme.

Leather goods

Rue Tronchet, rue St-Lazare and adjacent streets (*métro: St-Lazare*), boulevard St-Michel and nearby (*métro: St-Michel*), rue des Archives, Marais (*métro: Hôtel de Ville*).

Luxury goods

Rue Royale (china, crystal), Champs Elysées (perfumes).

Fashion

For most people, Paris fashion suggests a dreamworld of elegance, refinement, fantasy and originality that has helped create the glamorous image of the French capital.

Only a few designers and creators belong to the exclusive club of *haute couture* (literally 'high dressmaking') whose very existence depends on the collections. These are feverishly prepared in great secrecy and revealed during ritual fashion shows in January and June for designer clothes, March and October for *prêt-à-porter* (ready-to-wear). The media plays an essential role in these sophisticated 'performances', in which the top models are the stars. The designers create made-to-measure, very expensive outfits for a mainly foreign clientele. Behind the scenes, a whole army of *petites mains* (seamstresses), embroiderers, milliners and so on works endless hours to realise the masterpieces. The creators, on the other hand, concentrate their efforts on *prêt-à-porter*, accessories and perfumes, initiating new styles and trends that are copied by clothes manufacturers everywhere.

Well apart from the glittering world of designer clothes, the Sentier district (rue Réaumur and side streets, métro Sentier) houses a thousand or so stylists who are in direct contact with retail shops, and who test a limited number of designs. They then mass-produce the most successful ones in the space of a few days.

Major projects are under consideration to consolidate the success of the lucrative but vulnerable fashion industry. A *maison de la mode* (headquarters of fashion) has been built under the place du Carrousel at the Louvre, and there are plans for a *cité internationale de la mode* near La Villette. However, above all, several specialised schools ensure that the young designers of tomorrow are being trained to follow in the footsteps of Cardin, Givenchy, Yves St-Laurent, Christian Dior, Chanel, and a score of household names that, despite repeated offensives from Milan, New York, London and Tokyo, have maintained Paris as the uncontested world capital of fashion.

Paris chic – enviable, inimitable – embodied by its women, its designers, its models

Le Champo, the well-loved Latin Quarter cinema

Entertainment

There are numerous opportunities for entertainment of every kind, whether cultural or not, for the whole family, or for adults only, by day or by night.

WHAT'S ON

The Office du Tourisme et des Congrès de Paris brings out two publications: an annual one called *Saisons de Paris*, which lists the main events (festivals, exhibitions, concerts, etc); and the more detailed monthly, *Paris Sélection*, which has a special section devoted to young people, some useful addresses, and shopping suggestions.

You can also ring **Paris Sélection Loisirs** (*tel: 01 49 52 53 56*) at any time of day or night to get pre-recorded weekly information in English. Furthermore, there are two excellent weekly publications in French (both out on Wednesday): *Pariscope* and *L'Officiel des Spectacles*. They include up-to-date admission charges, and a special listing of restaurants open after midnight and on Sundays.

Tickets

Tickets for the theatre, concerts and other shows can be obtained directly or from the agencies listed below, through whom advance bookings can be made from abroad. This is strongly recommended as performances can be booked up very quickly.

Spectaplus, *252 rue du Faubourg St-Honoré, 75008. Tel: 01 53 53 58 60; fax: 01 53 53 58 61. Métro: Charles-de-Gaulle-Etoile.*

FNAC Billeterie, all over Paris. *Tel: 08 03 80 88 03.*
Agence Perrosier, *6 place de la Madeleine, 75008. Tel: 01 42 60 58 31; fax: 01 42 60 14 83. Métro: Madeleine.*
Virgin Megastore, *52–60 Champs Elysées, 75008. Tel: 01 49 53 52 09. Métro: Franklin-Roosevelt.*

Half-price tickets for performances the same day are available from the following kiosks (*open: Tue–Sat 12.30–7.45pm, Sun 12.30–4pm*): *15 place de la Madeleine, 75008. Métro: Madeleine; Esplanade de la Tour Montparnasse, 75015. Métro: Montparnasse Bienvenue.*

Cinemas

Cinemas are a popular form of entertainment in Paris, and film reviews regularly merit extensive coverage in the weekly 'what's on' publications. There is always a good choice of new releases, called *exclusivités*, and of old films, called *reprises*, often shown *en version originale* – *V.O.* for short (meaning in the original language) – particularly on the Champs Elysées, in the Latin Quarter, in the Odéon district and at the complex at Bercy Village.

Large cinemas have several auditoriums, each showing a different film; for instance, the George V at 144 and 146 avenue des Champs Elysées has no fewer than 11 auditoriums, the Gaumont Ambassade at No 50 has seven, and there are several other multiple cinemas along the 'Champs', as well as three in the Forum des Halles.

Some cinemas go in for festivals devoted to famous directors or actors: for instance, 'Hommage à Frank Capra', 'La Légende Bogart' or 'Viva James Bond!'. Classics are shown in the *cinémathèques* of the Palais de Chaillot and Palais de Tokyo (*métro: Trocadéro*), and in the Centre Pompidou (*métro: Rambuteau*), while the *vidéothèque* of the Forum des Halles (*métro: Les Halles*) mainly shows documentaries.

In most cinemas prices are reduced on Mondays. On other days children, students and sometimes senior citizens are entitled to a reduction.

Theatres

The most prestigious of them all, the Comédie Française, also called Le Théâtre Français or simply Le Français (*1 place de la Comédie Française, 75001, tel: 01 44 58 15 15*; *métro: Palais-Royal. Also see pp94–5*), traditionally puts on the great French classical comedies and tragedies by Molière, Racine and other masters. Its repertoire also includes selected 20th-century French and foreign plays. The acting is usually superb. The following theatres put on good productions of modern French and foreign plays. Booking starts two weeks in advance.

L'Atelier
Place Charles-Dullin, 75018.
Tel: 01 46 06 49 24. Métro: Anvers.
Cartoucherie (Théâtre du Soleil)
Route du Champ-des-Manoeuvres, 75012.

Tel: 01 43 74 99 61.
Métro: Château de Vincennes, then shuttle service.
Comédie des Champs-Elysées
15 avenue Montaigne, 75008. Tel: 01 53 23 99 19. Métro: Alma-Marceau.
Espace Marais
22 rue Beautreillis, 75004.
Tel: 01 48 04 91 55. Métro: St-Paul.
Hébertot
78 bis boulevard des Batignolles, 75017.
Tel: 01 43 87 23 23. Métro: Villiers, Rome.
Huchette
Eugène Ionesco plays.
23 rue de la Huchette, 75005.
Tel: 01 43 26 38 99. Métro: St-Michel.
Lucernaire Centre National d'Art et d'Essai
53 rue Notre-Dame-des-Champs, 75006.
Tel: 01 45 44 57 34. Métro: Vavin.
Poche Montparnasse
75, boulevard de Montparnasse, 75006.
Tel: 01 45 48 91 97. Métro: Montparnasse Bienvenue.
Théâtre National de Chaillot
1 place du Trocadéro, 75016.
Tel: 01 53 65 30 00. Métro: Trocadéro.

Paris offers many choices to cinema-goers

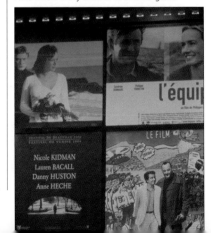

Café life

The French café is an institution; it is not a bar, that is not subtle enough, it is not a pub, that is not Latin enough, it is not a wine bar either, although it does sell wine. In a word, the French café is unique. Most visitors to France know that, and their faces light up at the thought of indulging an hour or two sitting on the crowded terrace of a café watching the world go by.

Cafés are busy all day. They open early in the morning in time to serve the traditional *grand crème* (large cup of white coffee) with croissants to people on their way to work. Throughout the day they serve wine by the glass, beer – *un demi* (originally ½ litre, just over a pint), or *une pression* (a glass of draught beer) – or *un pastis*, a strong aniseed drink diluted with water, and, of course, the tiny *espresso*, a cup of strong black coffee that seems to keep French people going. Drinks are cheaper *au bar* (standing at the bar) than *en salle* (sitting at one of the typical round tables). You can always spot the waiters and waitresses, wearing the traditional black and white uniform, as they make their way through the crowd with great agility.

The local cafés, where 'regulars' have their drink at 11am, working people eat a quick snack at lunchtime, and local residents meet in the evening to catch up on the news, play an important role in the city's social life. They have nothing in common with the elegant establishments of the place de l'Opéra, full of wealthy tourists and retired Parisians, or even with the Left Bank cafés where a fashionable élite goes to be seen.

Variety in an unpressured atmosphere: a leisurely *petit déjeuner*, a mid-morning pick-me-up, a range of hot options, an observation post on society

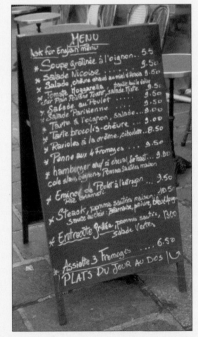

Music

As soon as the season ends in June, festivals take over, so that there is always a wide choice of concerts.

Classical concerts

Paris has many orchestras, from the chamber ensemble to the symphony orchestra. The most prestigious are the Orchestre National de France, the Orchestre Philharmonique de Radio France, the Orchestre de Paris and the Ensemble Intercontemporain. The main venues vary in size from the small **Salle Gaveau** to the vast **Théâtre des Champs Elysées** and the **Salle Pleyel**. There are lunchtime or early evening concerts in many churches throughout the capital, concerts in parks and gardens from May to September, and an enterprising operation, *Monuments en Musique*, which provides short musical programmes at regular intervals in selected monuments.

Opera and ballet

Most major operas are now staged at the **Opéra Bastille**, but the **Opéra Garnier** seems to be getting its share again, when technical conditions permit. The rest of the time it is the exclusive home of ballet. The Orchestre de l'Opéra de Paris, which is shared between the two houses, is one of the top orchestras in the country.

Jazz, rock and pop music

Concerts are usually held in large venues such as the **Zénith** at La Villette (*see p117*), the **Palais Omnisports Paris Bercy** (*boulevard de Bercy, 75012; métro: Bercy*) and the **Palais des Congrès** (*Porte Maillot, 75017; métro: Porte-Maillot*). The old **Olympia** music hall (*boulevard des Capucines, 75009; métro: Opéra*) is the traditional venue for variety shows, and all aspiring artists hope to top the bill there.

Nightlife

Like most capital cities, Paris has a large number of bars, discos, nightclubs and sex shows (the latter mainly in the sleazy Pigalle area), but its cabaret shows are still considered the most typically French form of night entertainment.

Cabarets

These became famous at the turn of the 20th century, partly for their lavish, colourful productions and partly because they shocked the predominantly bourgeois society. Today they no longer shock, but the productions are just as lavish.

Moulin Rouge

The most famous, with its 'girls' dancing the French cancan.
82 boulevard de Clichy, 75018.
Tel: 01 53 09 82 82.
Métro: Blanche.

Folies Bergère
32 rue Richer, 75009.
Tel: 01 44 79 98 98.
Métro: Grands Boulevards or Cadet.

Lido

Very sophisticated light effects.
116 bis avenue des Champs Elysées, 75008.
Tel: 01 40 76 56 10.
Métro: George V.

Crazy Horse Saloon

Reputed to be the most erotic of all.
12 avenue George V, 75008.

Tel: 01 47 23 32 32.
Métro: George V.

Jazz clubs
Very popular, also very crowded; arrive early but don't expect things to get going before 11pm.
Au Duc des Lombards
Small, cosy club.
42 rue des Lombards, 75001.
Tel: 01 42 33 22 88.
Métro: Chalet-les-Halles.
Bilboquet
Jazz club in *belle-époque* setting.
13 rue St-Benoit, 75006.
Tel: 01 45 48 81 84.
Métro: St-Germain-des-Prés.
Caveau de la Huchette
Authentic jazz cellar with dancing (rock 'n' roll) to live bands.
5 rue de la Huchette, 75005.
Tel: 01 43 26 65 05.
Métro: St-Michel.
La Villa
Chic and cosy jazz club in small St-Germain-des-Prés hotel.

The famous Moulin Rouge

29 rue Jacob, 75006.
Tel: 01 43 26 60 00. Métro: St-Germain-des-Prés.
New Morning
Jazz and world music venue featuring internationally acclaimed musicians.
7–9 rue des Petites-Ecuries, 75010.
Tel: 01 45 23 51 41.
Métro: Château-d'eau.
Petit Journal Montparnasse
Blues, African and traditional jazz.
13 rue du Commandant, Mouchotte, 75014.
Tel: 01 43 21 56 70.
Métro: Gaîté.

Nightclubs
These liven up from midnight onwards.
Les Bains
Nightclub in old public baths.
7 rue du Bourg-l'Abbé, 75003.
Tel: 01 48 87 01 80.
Métro: Etienne Marcel.
Le Niel's
Haunt of press and showbiz people.
27 avenue des Ternes, 75017.
Tel: 01 47 66 45 00.
Métro: Ternes.
La Loco
Trendy nightclub near Montmartre.
90 boulevard de Clichy, 75018.
Tel: 01 53 41 88 88.
Métro: Blanche.
La Scala
Special effects with laser lights.
188 bis rue de Rivoli, 75001.
Tel: 01 42 60 45 64.
Métro: Palais Royal or Tuileries.

Children

Paris and the Ile-de-France offer children of all ages a choice of entertaining activities, whatever the weather.

Monuments
A climb up the Eiffel Tower will thrill youngsters of all ages, while older ones will enjoy the Conciergerie and its gruesome stories, the Château de Vincennes and Versailles.

Museums
The **Musée Grévin** in the boulevard Montmartre, with its wax figures of famous historical and contemporary characters, is both entertaining and educational (*see p86*).

Many museums organise special activities for children of different age groups; the **Cité des Sciences et de l'Industrie** at la Villette (*see pp116–17*) offers an introduction to science and technology called **Cité des Enfants** with workshops for 3- to 5- and 6- to 12-year-olds; robots, computers and audio-visual games encourage children to participate, and there are special shows at the planetarium.

A moment of contemplation in the Jardin des Tuileries: the parks are enjoyed by all ages

The Centre Georges Pompidou (*see pp36–7*) aims to help children discover art through workshops based on current exhibitions.

The **Louvre** (*see pp64–7*) has many workshops and tours aimed specifically at children, so contact the museum for current activities.

The **Palais de la Découverte** (*see p26*) has fascinating and easy-to-understand science exhibitions and interactive demonstrations.

THE WORLD OF THE SEA
Tropical Aquarium
293 avenue Daumesnil, 75012. Tel: 01 43 46 51 61. Open: Wed–Mon 10am–5.15pm. Closed: Tue. Admission charge. Métro: Porte Dorée.

L'Argonaute
A real submarine and exhibition at the *Cité de Sciences et de l'Industrie at La Villette, 30 avenue Corentin-Cariou, 75019. Tel: 01 40 05 83 28. Open: Tue–Sat 10am–6pm, Sun 10am–7pm. Closed: Mon. Admission charge. Métro: Porte de la Villette.*

Centre de la Mer et des Eaux
At this marine and freshwater centre, simple phenomena are explained through observation, games and audio-visual presentations.
195 rue St-Jacques, 75005. Tel: 01 44 32 10 70. Open: Tue–Fri 10am–12.30pm & 1.30–5.30pm, Sat & Sun 10am–5.30pm.

Closed: Mon, and Sat & Sun in Aug.
Admission charge. Métro: Luxembourg.

PARKS AND GARDENS
Jardin d'Acclimatation
In the Bois de Boulogne this is an
amusement park for children of all ages.
A little train dating from 1878 (first
used at the Paris Exhibition of that year)
runs a shuttle service between the Porte
Maillot station and the park every
20 minutes or so from 10.15am. Other
attractions include an enchanted house,
miniature golf, an open-air circus and a
puppet theatre.
Bois de Boulogne, 75016. Tel: 01 40 67
90 82. Open: 10am–6pm (7pm summer).
Admission charge. Métro: Porte Maillot
(little train) or Sablons.

Jardin du Luxembourg
Adventure playgrounds, puppet shows
and toy wooden yachts for hire to sail
on the central pond.
Rue de Médicis, 75005.
RER: Luxembourg.

While most parks in the capital have a
children's play area, three are better
equipped. The **Parc des Buttes-
Chaumont** (*see p140*) has lots of space
and plenty of attractions, including
rock-climbing for older children. The
Parc Georges Brassens (*see p140*) has
wooden huts in a miniature forest
setting with rocks to match, as well as
the usual attractions. **The Parc Floral de
Paris** in the Bois de Vincennes (*see
p123*) aims to initiate children in the
pleasures of a nature trail.

Zoos
There is a small zoo in the **Jardin des**

The perfect mixture: kids and open space

Plantes (*see p140*) and another in the
Bois de Vincennes (*see p123*).

FUN WITH WATER
Aquaboulevard
An aquatic adventure playground. It
offers such attractions as giant slides and
a bubble pool.
4 rue Louis-Armand, 75015. Tel: 01 40 60
10 00. Open: Mon–Thur 9am–11pm,
Fri–Sat 9am–midnight, Sun 8am–11pm.
Admission charge. Métro: Balard.

   In fine weather, children will enjoy
a boat trip on the **Lac Inférieur** in the
Bois de Boulogne or on the **Lac
Daumesnil** in the Bois de Vincennes,
and also a trip on the Seine in one of the
Bateaux Mouches boats (*see p186*).

Shows
There are *Guignol* (Punch and Judy)
shows in most public parks and gardens.
Paris also has a number of circuses
which move about according to the
season. Ring the following for the latest
information on performances:
Cirque Bouglione, *tel: 01 47 00 12 25.*
Cirque Bormann, *tel: 01 48 39 04 47.*
Cirque Gruss, *tel: 01 40 36 08 00.*

Sport and leisure

Regular television coverage of sports events has contributed to a change of attitude towards sport in France, and particularly in Paris. Sport has entered every home, and the number of spectators has reached phenomenal proportions. As a result, more money has been invested in making sport accessible to a wider public. Stadiums and large indoor venues have been modernised, and facilities for individual sports have improved.

Stade Roland-Garros

Sports centres and stadiums

More than 500 national and international sports events take place every year in the city's main venues. Built in 1984, **Palais Omnisports Paris-Bercy** is a huge, multi-purpose centre; the seating capacity can be adapted to each event, with a maximum of 17,000. There is also an ice-skating rink, numerous dressing rooms and a medical centre. It is also frequently used for rock concerts (*8 boulevard de Bercy, 75012; tel: 01 40 02 60 60; métro: Bercy*).

Opened in 1998 with a capacity of 80,000 spectators, the **Stade de France** is the main venue for international football and rugby matches (*Zac du Cornillon Nord, Saint-Denis 93216; métro: Saint Denis – Porte de Paris*). **The Parc des Princes** is home to Paris-St-Germain FC (*24 rue du Commandant-Guilbaud, 75016; métro: Exelmans or Porte de St-Cloud*).

Quite close is the famous **Stade Roland-Garros**, which stages the annual French Open tennis competition. The tennis complex has 16 courts, including a centre court with room for 16,500

spectators (*2 avenue Gordon-Bennett, 75016; tel: 01 47 43 48 00; métro: Porte d'Auteuil*). Next to it, on the edge of the Bois de Boulogne, are two of Paris's three racecourses: the **Hippodrome d'Auteuil** (*champs de course d'Auteuil; tel: 01 40 71 47 47; métro: Porte d'Auteuil*), famous for steeplechasing, and the **Hippodrome de Longchamp** (*route des Tribunes, Bois de Boulogne, 75116; tel: 01 44 30 75 00; métro: Porte d'Auteuil, then shuttle bus*). The third racecourse is the **Hippodrome de Vincennes** on the other side of town (*2 route de la Ferme, 75012; tel: 01 49 77 17 17; RER: Joinville-le-Pont*).

In the 16th *arrondissement*, the **Stade Pierre de Coubertin** stages events such as judo and fencing competitions, gymnastics and dance displays, boxing and basketball matches (*82 avenue Georges-Lafont, 75016; tel: 01 45 27 79 12; métro: Porte de St-Cloud*).

The Stade Georges Carpentier holds indoor sports competitions such as martial arts, volleyball, badminton and table tennis (*81 boulevard Masséna, 75013; tel: 01 42 16 66 00;*

métro: Porte d'Ivry or Porte de Choisy).

The vast new **Stade Charléty**, with a capacity of 20,000 spectators, hosts both outdoor and indoor sports, from football to athletics, and tennis (*99 bd Kellerman, 75013; tel: 01 44 16 60 60; métro: Cité Universitaire*).

Built for the 1924 Olympic Games, the **Georges Vallerey swimming pool** saw Johnny Weissmüller of Tarzan fame beat the world 400m freestyle record. Entirely modernised in 1989, it can now hold water polo events, as well as international swimming competitions (*148 avenue Gambetta, 75020; tel: 01 40 31 15 20; métro: Porte des Lilas*).

SPECTATOR SPORTS
Cycling
The colourful and often dramatic finish of the Tour de France is staged along the Champs Elysées.

Football
The final of the Coupe de France is usually held in Paris in April or May.

Racing
There are two racecourses on the south side of the Bois de Boulogne. Auteuil specialises in steeplechasing and is famous for its difficult jumps. Flat racing takes place at Longchamp. Prestigious races such as the Prix du Président de la République on Palm Sunday, or the Grand Prix de l'Arc de Triomphe on the first Sunday in October, draw fashionable crowds who come more to be seen than to watch the racing. The Vincennes racecourse, situated on the other side of town, is popular for trotting events.

Rugby
France's home games in the Tournoi des Six Nations, involving England, Scotland, Wales, Ireland, France and Italy, are held at the Stade de France.

Running
The famous Marathon de Paris takes place in the capital in March or April.

Tennis
The Championnats Internationaux de France (French Open) take place at the Stade Roland-Garros in late May and early June. The Open de la Ville de Paris is held in the Palais Omnisports de Paris-Bercy in late October.

In the footsteps of heroes: volleyball in the park

PARTICIPATORY SPORTS

There are more than 250 locations all over Paris where amateurs and professionals can practise the sport of their choice. Municipal equipment is available to everyone for a very modest fee, and visitors may join certain private clubs on a temporary basis.

To get the best information on what is available in your area, contact the Office Municipal des Sports in the *mairie d'arrondissement* (district town hall). You can also obtain from the *mairie* a booklet entitled *Centre d'Animation Magazine,* published twice yearly, which contains a list of all sports centres, with addresses and programmes. *Sport à la carte* has been specially devised to provide individual programmes in municipal centres at fixed hours.

Climbing

Three new structures have been installed in the city to accommodate the growing number of enthusiasts; the most impressive is located at the
Stade des Poissonniers
2 rue Jean-Cocteau, 75018. Tel: 01 42 51 24 68. Open: daily 7.30am–10pm. Sun 8am–6pm. Maximum height: 21m (70 ft). Métro: Porte de Clignancourt.

For other possibilities and information contact the Fédération Française de la Montagne et de l'Escalade (*8–10 quai de la Marne, 75008, tel: 01 40 18 75 50*).

Cycling

Nearly 400 clubs in the Paris region organise tours in Ile-de-France. For information contact:

Fédération Française de Cyclisme
5 rue de Rome, 75008.
Tel: 01 49 35 69 00.

Golf

Several clubs and centres offer golfers the possibility of practising putting, and even their drive, with the help of simulators. However, the real thing takes place out of town. For detailed information contact:
Fédération Française de Golf
68 Anatole France, Levallois Perret, 92300. Tel: 01 41 49 77 00.

Gymnastics and fitness

Many clubs specialise in keep-fit classes, aerobics, body-building, swimming, etc. Equipped with saunas and Jacuzzis, they are usually restricted 'members only' clubs. One of the most sophisticated is:
Espace Vit'Halles
48 rue Rambuteau, 75003.
Tel: 01 42 77 21 71. Métro: Rambuteau.

Swimming

There are many municipal swimming pools in Paris as well as a number of private ones. They are usually crowded. These are the most attractive:
Piscine des Halles
An Olympic-size pool with a view of the tropical glasshouse.
Forum des Halles. Level 3.
Tel: 01 42 36 98 44. Métro: Les Halles.
Piscine Jean Taris
Lovely Japanese garden setting.
16 rue Thouin, 75005. Tel: 01 55 42 81 90. Métro: Cardinal-Lemoine.
Piscine Pontoise
19 rue de Pontoise, 75005.

Tel: 01 55 42 77 88.
Métro: Maubert-Mutualité.

Tennis and squash

There are 150 municipal tennis courts open until 10pm, available by the hour at very reasonable fees. For detailed information, contact the local *mairie* (town hall) or Allo Sports (*see p188*). In addition, there are several private clubs:

Squash Montmartre
Four courts, clubhouse, restaurant.
14 rue Achille Martinet, 75018.
Tel: 01 42 55 38 30. Métro: Lamarck.

Squash Rennes Raspail
Seven courts and golf practice.
149 rue de Rennes, 75006.
Tel: 01 45 44 24 35. Métro: Rennes.

Tennis de Longchamp
Twenty courts.
19 boulevard Anatole-France, 92
Boulogne. Tel: 01 46 03 84 49.
Métro: Porte d'Auteuil.

Tenpin Bowling

This has been popular with young people for some time, more as a leisure activity than a sport.

Bowling Champerret
Place Porte Champerret, 75017. Tel: 01 43 80 24 64. Open: daily 10am–2am. Bar. Métro: Porte de Champerret.

Bowling Foch
2 bis avenue Foch, 75016.
Tel: 01 45 00 00 13. Open: daily 11am–2am. Bar. Métro: Etoile.

Bowling Montparnasse
27 rue Commandant René Mouchotte, 75014. Tel: 01 43 21 61 32. Open: daily 10am–2am (4am on Fri & Sat). Bar-restaurant.
Métro: Montparnasse.

Watersports

Waterskiing and canoeing are now possible at the new **Bassin de la Villette**
5 bis quai de la Loire, 75019;
métro: Jaurès or Stalingrad.

Leisure parks outside Paris

Activities include swimming, sailing, windsurfing, riding and tennis.
Base de Loisirs, Torcy, Marne-la-Vallée, route de Lagny
77 Torcy. 25km (15¹/₂ miles) east of Paris. Tel: 01 64 80 58 75. Open: 9am–6pm. RER: Torcy-Marne-la-Vallée.
Le Val de Seine
78480 Verneuil-sur-Seine. 30km (18 miles) west of Paris. Tel: 01 39 71 07 06. Open: 9am–noon, 2–6pm.

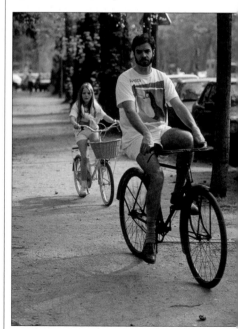

Cycling in the Bois de Boulogne

Food and drink

Food is an important ingredient of the French way of life and some of the rituals that accompany its preparation and consumption are still performed by a majority of French people, even in Paris where the pressures of modern city life seem to go against the more traditional principles of gastronomy.

Garlic is a staple of French cuisine

Eating habits

The French are particular about 'fresh' food: bread, meat and vegetables are usually bought daily. A lot of people shop after working hours, which explains why food shops and markets stay open late. The time spent on cooking varies, but has been considerably shortened for working people, thanks to the mouth-watering, freshly prepared dishes sold in the numerous *charcuteries*.

Although two main meals a day is usual, around midday and 8pm, in Paris lunch tends to be reduced to a quick light meal, the emphasis being on the evening meal served with wine. A family meal generally comprises one type of wine, usually red, though special meals include at least two different wines, carefully chosen to go with each dish. Some people drink beer with their meals, and nearly everyone drinks mineral water and fruit juice some time during the day. Breakfast is not very copious: freshly bought bread with butter and jam, marmalade or honey, and/or a croissant. *Boulangeries* open early so people can drop in for fresh supplies before going to work. *Café au lait*, or *café crème* (white coffee) as it is

called in cafés, is still the popular breakfast drink, but more people are drinking black coffee these days, and tea is gaining in popularity.

Shopping for food

Food shops have a place of honour in the best districts, and some of them have elaborate, imaginative displays worthy of shops selling luxury goods – that is exactly what they are doing.

Shopping streets and markets

Each district has an open-air market as well as one or two streets, often pedestrianised during part of the day, where food shops are concentrated and stalls are set up on the pavement to promote certain kinds of produce. Prices can vary considerably; the accent is on friendliness, and customers are invited to select what they want. Basic shops always include one or two *boucheries* (butchers), *boulangeries-pâtisseries* (bakers), *crèmeries-fromageries* (dairies), *charcuteries* (delicatessens) and *poissonneries* (fishmongers).

The following streets are renowned for good quality and good value:
Near Les Halles: the rue Montorgueil, which still keeps alive the atmosphere of

the old Les Halles central food market (*see p54*), and the rue Rambuteau.

In the 17th arrondissement: the rue Poncelet near the place des Ternes, where there is one of the best coffee shops in Paris, the Brûlerie des Ternes at No 10, and the rue de Lévis near the Parc Monceau.

On the Left Bank: the rue Mouffetard, the rue de Buci and the rue de Seine, probably the most picturesque in Paris.

Specialised shops

Cheese can be bought in supermarkets, *épiceries* (grocers) and from market stalls. However, connoisseurs prefer to select from one of the more than 500 different cheeses made in France, buying from a reputed *fromager* who can recommend the best *brebis* (ewes' milk cheese), the tastiest *chevrotin* (goats' milk cheese from Savoie) or a superb *Pont-l'Evêque* (a famous cows' milk cheese from Normandy).

Androuët (*41 rue d'Amsterdam, 75008; métro: Liège*) is something of a legend, with over 200 varieties kept at the right temperature in the cellars. **Lionel Poilâne** (*8 rue du Cherche-Midi, 75006; métro: Sèvres-Babylone*), adept at authenticity, is undoubtedly the most famous bakery in Paris, while the *pâtisserie* **Lenôtre** (*48 avenue Victor-Hugo, 75016; métro: Victor-Hugo*) is unequalled for imagination and refinement. **Berthillon** (*31 rue St-Louis-en-l'Ile, 75004; métro: Pont-Marie*) is the best place for ice cream, including many unusual flavours.

The Madeleine area (*métro: Madeleine*) has several luxury food shops, including the famous **Fauchon** (*26 place de la Madeleine*), an *épicerie fine* (luxury grocer) and delicatessen whose displays are real works of art, and the more modest **Hédiard** at No 21. Next door at No 19 is the **Maison de la Truffe**, where you can buy fresh truffles as well as delicious *charcuterie*. Nearby, in the rue Vignon, is the **Maison du Miel** at No 24, where you can taste and buy all kinds of rare honey.

Mixed salad: a range of fresh produce is on offer

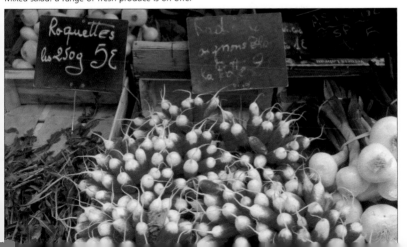

It is a well-known, although controversial, fact that 'Paris is not France'; the French themselves acknowledge it, especially if they are not Parisians. Yet, paradoxically, although there is no Parisian cuisine as such, Paris has become a melting pot of the best culinary traditions, and the undisputed capital of French gastronomy.

Variety is the first and foremost characteristic of French cuisine. The ingredients used in cooking have regional origins; cream, butter and cheese are widely used in northern areas where milk products are plentiful, while olive oil and garlic are typical of Mediterranean areas; red wine makes casseroles rich and tasty in the Bourgogne district.

The universal fame of traditional French cuisine rests on the variety of its regional dishes.

Among starters, you may find *hors-d'oeuvre variés* (raw vegetables seasoned with oil and vinegar, served with assorted *charcuterie*), *quiche lorraine* (savoury flan with pieces of

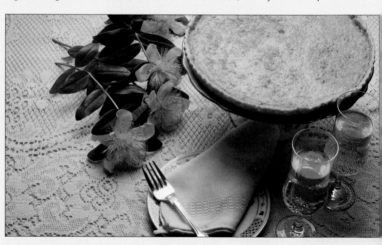

bacon), *moules marinière* (mussels simmered in white wine with shallots) or the delicious *soupe à l'onion gratinée* (onion soup with melted cheese).

Main dishes usually include several of the following: *entrecôte bordelaise* (juicy steak with a rich wine sauce), *boeuf bourguignon* (casseroled beef with onions and mushrooms, in a red Burgundy wine), *blanquette de veau* (stewed veal with cream and mushrooms) and *choucroute garnie* (sauerkraut cooked in dry white wine, with pork and sausages). *Gratin dauphinois* (sliced potatoes baked with cream and grated cheese) is ideal with tasty grills.

To finish a good meal, there is nothing more refreshing than a home-baked *crème caramel* (egg custard coated with caramel), or a cool *baba-au-rhum* (light sponge cake with rum syrup).

However, French cuisine does not rely for its success on tradition alone, for it is constantly being reinvented and perfected by ambitious young chefs whose imagination has no bounds.

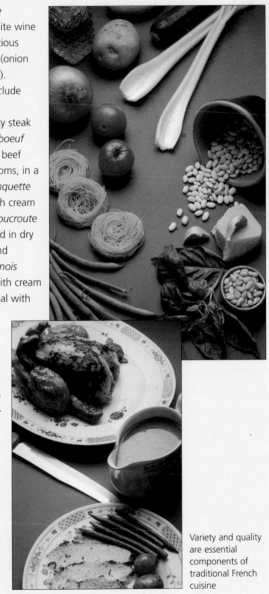

Variety and quality are essential components of traditional French cuisine

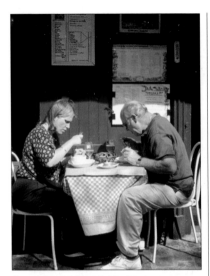

Casual alfresco dining in Montmartre

Eating out

The choice is vast and there are places to suit every occasion, from local, inexpensive *bistros* to exclusive temples of gastronomy, from fast-food bars and quaint tearooms to regional and exotic ethnic restaurants.

Each type of establishment has its own personality and represents a different aspect of Parisian life. Crowded at lunchtime, cafés are ideal for a quick meal, with a restricted menu usually consisting of *steak/frites* (steak and chips), mixed salads and a selection of sandwiches made with crisp *baguettes* (French bread). Slightly more expensive, *brasseries* offer a choice of traditional dishes that include an Alsatian *choucroute garnie* (sauerkraut with assorted sausages) served with beer or wine. Top *brasseries* have an attractive display of fresh seafood just outside

their premises with an attendant serving oysters and other pricey delicacies to passers-by and preparing orders for customers inside. There are several such establishments on the place de Clichy, not far from the Moulin Rouge.

Wine bars are not steeped in tradition like cafés and *brasseries*, but they seem to fit in well with the Parisians' changing lifestyle, and are becoming increasingly popular as a lunchtime venue. They serve an assortment of cold platters and cheese with selected wines by the glass, thus enabling the real amateur to taste and enjoy excellent wine without having to buy a full bottle. **L'Ecluse** (*15 quai des Grands-Augustins, 75006; métro: St-Michel*) is one of the most famous, and a good place to sample for atmosphere.

Little known or talked about are the discreet but charming *salons de thé* (tearooms), often tucked away in picturesque arcades. They offer the luxury of a relaxed atmosphere in refined surroundings, and serve good-quality snacks and pastries with a choice of fine teas or coffee. Two of the best are **Angélina** (*226 rue de Rivoli, near the Jardin des Tuileries*) and **La Cour de Rohan** (*Cour du Commerce St-André, off the rue St-André-des-Arts, near the place St-Michel*).

The name restaurant applies to a wide range of establishments, from the unassuming, friendly, local place with white lace curtains at the windows and rickety tables outside in summertime, to the select, fashionable, outrageously expensive, or just exquisitely refined rendezvous for gourmets. The variety stems from the type of cuisine served, whether French or ethnic. Typical cuisines from the regions of France are well represented by authentic chefs who have come to the capital to make a name for themselves. In some cases they are concentrated in a specific area. For instance, exponents of Breton cuisine are grouped in the vicinity of the Gare Montparnasse, while specialities from the Auvergne are to be found in the Bastille area.

The number of ethnic restaurants has increased lately and they, too, tend to congregate in specific areas, sometimes taking over a whole street, like the rue de la Huchette, near the place St-Michel, which is lined with cheap Greek and North African restaurants. The rue des Rosiers and adjacent streets in the Marais are well known for their Jewish and East European restaurants. The 13th *arrondissement*, near the Porte d'Ivry, where Asian restaurants are plentiful, has been christened 'Chinatown'. By contrast, you hardly notice the less conspicuous presence of several Japanese restaurants in the Opéra district.

Choosing a restaurant

It is difficult to generalise about value for money as quality and prices vary a lot. On the whole, however, one may say that, in the lower price range, value for money – both in quantity and quality – is better in Paris than in most Western capitals. This tends to be less true in the upper price range, but Paris still retains a slight advantage as far as service, attention to detail, and imagination are concerned.

The price range given in the listings below refers to an average meal per person, not including drinks. There are four categories:

★	Less than €30
★★	€30–€45
★★★	€45–€75
★★★★	More than €75

The restaurants selected are in the nine areas covered most extensively in this book. Most are closed on Sundays.

Vegetarian food

Vegetarians may struggle a little in Paris as French cuisine is very strongly meat-based. Although vegetarianism is regarded as a kind of eccentricity, almost everywhere will have a range of salads and maybe pasta dishes – but watch out for salads with bacon in!

Rabbit, anyone? Lapin Agile, Montmartre

Where to eat
MARAIS, ILE ST-LOUIS
Au C'Amelot ★
Romantic stone-walled
room where the chef's
market-based menu is
imaginative, though
limited to two choices
per course.
50 rue Amelot, 75011.
Tel: 01 43 55 54 04.
Métro: Chemin Vert.

**Nos Ancêtres les
Gaulois ★**
Four courses for a fixed
price and unlimited
wine in a convivial
pseudo-medieval setting.
39 rue St-Louis-en-l'Ile,
75004. Tel: 01 46 33 66 07.
Métro: Pont-Marie.

Le Pamphlet ★★
Affordable sophistication
in this fashionable
restaurant where you'll
need to book ahead to
sample the inventive
modern cuisine.
38 rue Debelleyme, 75003.
Tel: 01 42 72 39 24.
Métro: Filles du Calvaire.

LES HALLES
Au Pied de Cochon ★
An old classic from
market days at Les Halles.
Serves traditional onion
soup. Good place for pigs'
trotters.
6 rue Coquillière, 75001.
Tel: 01 42 36 11 75.
Métro: Les Halles.

Gérard Besson ★★★
Authentic gourmet
cuisine; elegant décor.
5 rue du Coq-Héron,
75001. Tel: 01 42 33 14 74.
Métro: Louvre.

Potager du Marais ★
Constant glowing reports
make this vegetarian
(plus a few fish dishes)
option worth seeking out,
but take your phrase
book if you don't speak
good French.
22 rue Rambuteau, 75004.
Tel: 01 42 74 24 66.
Métro: Rambuteau.

PALAIS-ROYAL, OPERA, CONCORDE
Aux Lyonnais ★★
Lyon cooking Alain
Ducasse-style has locals
flocking to this *faux* 19th-
century Lyonnais
restaurant.
32 rue St-Marc, 75002.
Tel: 01 42 96 65 04.
Métro: Richelieu Drouot.

Chartier ★
Chartier is so old-
fashioned it's now
fashionably retro, and one
of the cheapest deals in
town. Steak frites and
other plain grub in a
workmanlike *fin-de-siècle*
setting.
7 rue du Faubourg
Montmartre, 75009.
Tel: 01 47 70 86 29.
Métro: Grands Boulevards.

Cibus ★★
Eat Italian in Paris? Yes,
when the food is as
authentic as this. The chef
recites the menu, but the
place is tiny so book.
5 rue Molière, 75001.
Tel: 01 42 61 50 19.
Métro: Pyramides.

ETOILE, CHAMPS ELYSEES
**Le Fouquet's-Barriere
★★★**
A rendezvous for film
stars and celebrities.
99 avenue des Champs-
Elysées, 75008.
Tel: 01 47 23 50 00.
Métro: George V.

**Le Bistrot d'à Côté
Flaubert ★★**
New chef-owner has
transformed this food
shop into a fine bistro.
10 rue Gustave-Flaubert,
75017. Tel: 01 42 67 05 81.
Métro: Courcelles.

Taillevent ★★★★
High-class cuisine. Book
months ahead.
15 rue Lamennais, 75008.
Tel: 01 44 95 15 01.
Métro: George V.

TROCADERO, PASSY
La Butte Chaillot ★★
Refined cuisine; striking
contemporary setting.
110 bis avenue Kléber,
75016. Tel: 01 47 27 88 88.
Métro: Trocadéro.

Alain Ducasse au Plaza Athénée ★★★★
Futuristic design. Inspired cuisine by a great chef.
25 avenue Montaigne, 75008. Tel: 01 53 67 65 00. Métro: Alma-Marceau.

L'Astrance ★★
A first-rate bistro with contemporary décor.
4 rue Beethoven, 75006. Tel: 01 40 50 84 40. Métro: Passy.

Le Petit Rétro ★
Suberb traditional cuisine served in a listed building with 1910 décor.
5 rue Mesnil, 75016. Tel: 01 44 05 06 05. Métro: Victor Hugo.

MONTMARTRE
L'Etrier ★★
Refined, traditional French cuisine; good value; book a table.
154 rue Lamarck, 75018. Tel: 01 42 29 14 01. Métro: Guy Môquet.

Le Moulin à Vins ★
Lively and rustic with succulent charcuterie.
6 rue Burq, 75008. Tel: 01 42 52 81 27. Métro: Abbesses.

Pétrelle ★
If you'll eat anything then Pétrelle's no-choice menu is a terrific deal, and you'll soon taste why the place has become a fashionable hang-out.
34 rue Pétrelle, 75009. Tel: 01 42 82 11 02. Métro: Anvers.

LATIN QUARTER
L'Atelier de Maître Albert ★★★
Fixed-price includes half a bottle of wine.
1 rue Maître-Albert, 75005. Tel: 01 56 81 30 01. Métro: Maubert-Mutualité.

La Tour d'Argent ★★★★
Expensive, excellent food.
15 quai de la Tournelle, 75005. Tel: 01 40 46 71 11. Métro: Maubert-Mutualité.

Le Grenier Notre-Dame ★
Vegetarian restaurant close to Notre-Dame.
18 rue de la Bûcherie, 75005. Tel: 01 43 29 98 29. Métro: Maubert-Mutualité.

ST-GERMAIN-DES-PRES
Aux Charpentiers ★
Publishers' haunt.
10 rue Mabillon, 75006. Tel: 01 43 26 30 05. Métro: Mabillon.

Les Bouquinistes ★★★
Fashionable restaurant along the embankment.
53 quai des Grands-Augustins, 75006. Tel: 01 43 25 45 94. Métro: St-Michel.

Jacques Cagna ★★★
Magnificent 17th-century house, excellent cuisine.
14 rue des Grands-Augustins, 75006. Tel: 01 43 26 49 39. Métro: St-Michel.

Le Petit Saint Benoit ★
Charming restaurant, simple, unpretentious home cooking.
4 rue Saint-Benoit, 75006. Tel: 01 42 60 27 92. Métro: St-Germain-des-Prés.

Le Petit Zinc ★★
Typical Left Bank bistro serving excellent seafood.
11 rue Saint-Benoit, 75006. Tel: 01 42 86 61 00. Métro: St-Germain-des-Prés.

Polidor ★
Authentic bistro with convivial atmosphere. Open till late.
41 rue Monsieur-le-Prince, 75006. Tel: 01 43 26 95 34. Métro: Luxembourg.

INVALIDES, FAUBOURG ST-GERMAIN
La Petite Chaise ★
Excellent value.
36 rue de Grenelle, 75007. Tel: 01 42 22 13 35. Métro: Sèvres-Babylone.

Le Divellec ★★★★
A top seafood restaurant.
107 rue de l'Université, 75007. Tel: 01 45 51 91 96. Métro: Invalides.

Vin sur Vin ★★
Close to the Eiffel Tower, copious savoury dishes.
20 rue de Monttessuy, 75007. Tel: 01 47 05 14 20. Métro: Pont de l'Alma.

Wines

Wine is the French national drink, its infinite variety matching that of French cuisine. Vines have been grown in France since Roman times, and ancestral traditions are still observed in many regions. Wine-making methods are strictly controlled, and a grading system is applied accordingly.

Vin de table is a cheap, ordinary wine. It is drunk 'young' (within a year). *Vin délimité de qualité supérieure* (VDQS) is a higher-grade wine that is produced in areas where quality is constant. *Appellation d'Origine Contrôlée* (AOC) denotes a wine characteristic of a specific district, or *cru*, such as Médoc in the Bordeaux region.

This information and more is on the labels, and it is well worth studying them carefully when selecting a good red or white château wine. Look for the year, as quality varies from year to year, and for the words *mis en bouteilles au château* (bottled at the château); but bear in mind that there are many château wines and the best of them have been graded as *cru bourgeois* and *grand cru* or *1er cru, 2ème cru*, and so on.

The two main wine-producing regions are the Bordeaux region in the southwest with famous wines like Médoc, Graves, St-Emilion or Pomerol, and Bourgogne in the east, with inspiring names such as Nuits-St-Georges, Chambertin, Pommard and Pouilly-Fuissé.

Other regions also produce some great wines; for instance, Châteauneuf-du-Pape, which comes from the Rhône

Valley, and Riesling from the Alsace. Champagne, named after the region in northeastern France, is in a class of its own. The lengthy production process was perfected in the 17th century by Dom Pérignon, a monk who came from the abbaye d'Hautvillers.

Wine-bottle shapes vary from one region to another, providing an immediate clue to their origins. Thus, the elegant, slim bottle from the southwest contrasts with the stockier type used in Bourgogne and Champagne, or the tall fluted ones typical of Alsace.

Whatever your taste, your budget or the occasion, there's a bottle of wine to suit it

Hotels and accommodation

Old and new, traditional and modern, Parisian hotels vary considerably in size and the degree of comfort they offer. During the last few years, many have been renovated, modernised and refurbished, with the emphasis on proper separate bathroom facilities instead of the usual washbasin and bidet, even in the lowest grade. Only the more expensive hotels have restaurants.

The highly fashionable Ritz hotel, Paris

Grading

The system used is the same as in other regions of France. Hotels are graded by the Direction de l'Industrie Touristique, according to the degree of comfort and quality of services. Present standards were fixed by decree in 1986, and regular checks are carried out by the Préfecture. There are five grades, which can be described as follows:

- HT, HRT, or 1-star applies to modest hotels with basic comforts, but bear in mind that standards have risen recently, although not necessarily everywhere.
- 2-star denotes a hotel, where you can expect a private bathroom.
- 3-star qualifies a very comfortable hotel, where a private bathroom and toilet are standard, and breakfast is served in the rooms if you so wish.
- 4-star is granted to high-class hotels. Some have long been internationally famous, such as the **Ritz**, *place Vendôme, 75001*; the **Crillon**, *place de la Concorde, 75008*; **the George V**, *avenue George V, 75008*; and the **Hilton Hotel Paris**, *avenue de Suffren, 75015*.

- 5-star is granted to only a very few de luxe hotels that the French call *palaces*. **The Meurice**, *rue de Rivoli, 75001*, was the German headquarters during World War II.

  As they are in greater demand, there are more 2- and 3-star hotels throughout the city.

Breakfast

As a rule, all hotels provide breakfast, but generally only 3-star and above offer room service. The price of breakfast is quoted separately from that of the room, and though you are expected to, you are not obliged to have it.

  In most cases, hotels offer a 'continental' breakfast, which usually includes tea, milk, coffee or chocolate, a *baguette* (crisp French bread) with butter and jam or honey, and croissants.

  Some hotels now offer an English- or American-style breakfast to guests on payment of a supplement.

Prices

By Western standards, Parisian hotels are fairly reasonably priced on the whole, although they are more expensive than in French provincial towns. Charging by the room rather than per person is still common practice (some hotels have family rooms for parents with one or two children).

Prices are not controlled, and so vary a lot according to the time of year, and even from one hotel to another within a given official category; they can also be changed without prior notice. However, prices including tax and service charge must be displayed outside hotels, in the reception area, and in the rooms.

The easiest method of payment is by credit card, which only a few hotels in the lowest category do not accept.

Selecting a hotel

Most people prefer central areas in order to reduce travelling times to a minimum and to be able fully to enjoy the atmosphere of the city. Most luxury hotels are in the Madeleine–Opéra–Champs Elysées area, which covers the 1st, 8th and 9th *arrondissements*, while the Left Bank, especially the 5th, 6th and 7th *arrondissements*, has a profusion of smaller, more relaxed, but still very comfortable, establishments. This is only a general indication and it is quite possible to find a middle- or lower-grade hotel on the Right Bank.

The convenience of central areas such as the Gare du Nord/Gare de l'Est, Pigalle and the eastern districts should be balanced against some less attractive aspects.

Hotels in Paris are listed in a free booklet published by the Office du Tourisme et des Congrès de Paris, which will be available from the official representative of the French tourist office in your country.

Comfort and convenience at the Hôtel Crillon, one of more than 1,400 hotels in the city

Booking a hotel

It is advisable to book in advance (preferably a month or so) all the year round, but especially between Easter and October when more tourists come to Paris. You can do so by telephone, e-mail, letter or fax. Make your preferences quite clear: a room at the back if traffic noise bothers you, a separate bathroom, or, if you don't like climbing stairs, inquire whether there is a lift or ask for a room on a lower floor. Normally, a deposit is required with your confirmation.

If you arrive in Paris without having made a reservation, the Office du Tourisme et des Congrès de Paris will be able to help you. They have a Service de Réservations Hôtelières in their main offices, located at *Carrousel du Louvre, 99 rue de Rivoli, tel: 08 92 68 30 00, www.parisinfo.com*, open daily from 10am to 6pm, and subsidiary offices at the main stations (except the Gare St-Lazare) as well as at the Eiffel Tower (from May to September only). These act as an emergency service for immediate accommodation, but they are closed on Sunday except at the Gare du Nord.

Below is a list of other organisations, *centrales de réservations hôtelières*, which deal with hotel bookings by phone or fax:
Abotel *Tel: 01 47 27 15 15; fax: 01 47 27 05 87. www.abotelparis.com*
Ely 12 12 *Tel: 01 43 59 12 12; fax: 01 42 56 24 31; www.ely1212.com*
Paris Séjour Réservation
Tel: 01 53 89 10 50; fax: 01 53 89 10 59.
Prestotel *Tel: 01 45 26 22 55; fax: 01 45 26 05 14.*

In the more upmarket establishments receptionists are usually bilingual, and any hotel with 2 or more stars must by law have a receptionist speaking a second language.

Other accommodation

Self-catering is ideal for those who wish to have complete freedom to sample French cuisine. Self-catering apartments on short-term lets, called *meublés de tourisme*, are available for a minimum of one week and for a maximum of three months. The fully furnished one- to four-room apartments are equipped with telephone, colour television and, in some cases, washing machine and dishwasher. Sheets are usually provided. Prices are lower for longer lets.

Below is a selection of agencies and organisations approved by the Office du Tourisme et des Congrès de Paris. They are usually open during normal office hours.
ABM Rent a Flat, *12 rue Valentin Haüy, 75015. Tel: 01 45 67 04 04; fax: 01 45 67 90 15. Métro: Ségur.*
Flatotel Expo, *52 rue d'Oradour sur Glane, 75015. Tel: 01 45 54 93 45; fax: 01 45 54 93 07.*
Métro: Porte de Versailles.
France-Ermitage, *5 rue Berryer, 75008. Tel: 01 42 56 23 42; fax: 01 42 56 08 99. Métro: Charles-de-Gaulle-Etoile or George V.*
Immovac, *37 avenue de Lowendal, 75015. Tel: 01 45 67 70 00; fax: 01 43 06 12 50. Métro: Cambronne.*
Alcove & Agapes, *8 bis rue Coysevox, 75018. Tel: 01 44 85 06 05; fax: 01 44 85 06 14; www.bedandbreakfastinparis.com. Métro: Guy Môquet.*

Bed and breakfast is ideal for those who wish to get to know French people and the French way of life. **Bed & Breakfast France** (*www.bedbreak.com; tel: 0871 781 0834 UK, 01 34 19 90 00 France*) offers a very good selection of Parisian hosts. A small booking fee is included in the price and it is advisable to book in advance.

For student accommodation and camping, *see p188 & p179*.

If you come to Paris by car you will encounter parking problems. Hotels with parking are generally modern blocks outside the centre, though many are located close to public car parks.

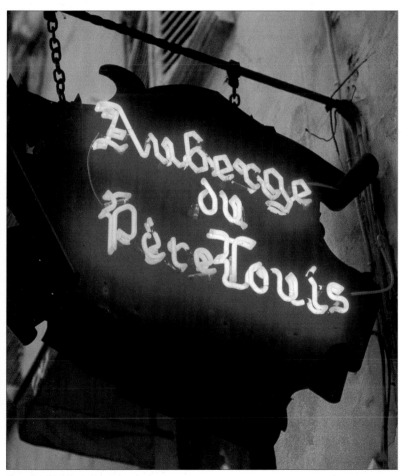

Sign of welcome at a Marais hotel

P r a c t i c a l   g u i d e

Arriving
EU residents visiting France need only show a valid passport to enter the country. This applies to US citizens, Canadians, Australians and New Zealand nationals also, providing the length of their stay does not exceed three months; a visa is required for a longer stay. Visas are obtainable from French embassies and consulates in your own country; apply two months in advance in case of delays.

By air
Paris has two main airports: Charles de Gaulle, 23km (14 miles) northeast of the city, and Orly, 14km (9 miles) south.

Charles de Gaulle (*tel: 01 48 62 22 80; 24 hours a day, www.adp.fr*). Roissyrail, the free airport shuttle bus service, takes passengers to Roissy station where they can board the RER B (train every 8 minutes) for Gare du Nord and Châtelet-les-Halles. Air France buses leave every 12–15 minutes to Porte Maillot, place Charles-de-Gaulle and Gare Montparnasse (from Terminal 2). Regular RATP buses also run from Roissy station to Gare du Nord/Gare de l'Est (No 350), and place de la Nation (No 351). The Roissy bus runs every 15 minutes from Terminal 2 to Opéra.

Orly (*tel: 01 49 75 15 15; 6am– midnight, www.adp.fr*). The new Orlyval fully automatic métro operates a shuttle service (every 10 minutes) between the airport and the RER B at Antony station, then on to Châtelet-les-Halles. It is more expensive than Orlyrail, which combines the airport bus shuttle service with the RER C to St-Michel-Notre-Dame (every 20 minutes). Air France buses leave every 12 minutes for Les Invalides and Gare Montparnasse. Orlybus runs every 15 minutes from the airport to the place Denfert-Rochereau, connecting with the RER B or the métro.

Almost every major national airline carrier in the world flies to Paris, most of them daily, so getting there by air is not a problem. Budget airlines serving Paris from the UK include easyJet (*www.easyjet.com*), bmibaby (*www.bmibaby.com*), flybe (*www.flybe.com*) and Ryanair (*www.ryanair.com*), though Ryanair flies to Paris Beauvais Airport, some 70km (43 miles) from the city centre.

By train
The six main-line stations are within easy reach of the city centre by RER or métro:

Gare d'Austerlitz *55 quai d'Austerlitz, 75013; RER C and métro line 10.*
Gare de l'Est *place du 11 novembre 1918, 75010; métro lines 4 and 7.*
Gare de Lyon *20 boulevard Diderot, 75012; RER A and métro line 1.*
Gare Montparnasse *17 boulevard de Vaugirard 75015; métro lines 4, 12 and 13.*
Gare du Nord *18 rue de Dunkerque, 75010; RER B and D and métro line 4.*
Gare St-Lazare *13 rue d'Amsterdam, 75008; RER E and métro line 14.* This station is situated in the centre, in the *Madeleine/Opéra* district.

Cross-Channel services from Britain arrive at *Gare du Nord* or *Gare St-Lazare*.

By car
Whether you arrive by *autoroute* (motorway) or *route nationale* (A road), you will meet the *boulevard périphérique*, which you can follow until you reach the *porte* (exit) closest to your destination.

Babysitter
Two reliable agencies are: **ABABA** (*tel: 01 45 49 46 46*) and **Allo! Service Maman** (*tel: 01 42 67 99 37*).

Camping
For information contact the **Fédération Française de Camping et de Caravanning** *78 rue de Rivoli, 75004* (*tel: 01 42 72 84 08, www.ffcc.fr*), *métro: Hôtel-de-Ville*.

The following are the most convenient camping sites in and around Paris: **Camping du Bois de Boulogne** (*Allée du Bord de l'Eau, 75016; tel: 01 45 24 30 00; métro: Pont-de-Neuilly, then bus No 244*); **Camping International** (*1 rue Johnson, 78600 Maisons-Lafitte; tel: 01 39 12 21 91; 15 minutes from Paris by RER A*); **Camping du Parc de Sejour de l'Étang** (*Base de Loisirs, 78180, Montigny-le-Bretonneux; tel: 01 30 58 56 20; RER C to St-Quentin-en-Yvelines*); **Camping du Parc de la Colline** (*route de Lagny, 77200 Torcy; tel: 01 60 05 42 32; RER A to Torcy-Marne-la-Vallée, then bus 421*).

Children
Children under four years travel free on the Paris transport network, and under-18s get into national museums free. Shoppers will find that baby food and disposable nappies are cheaper in large supermarkets than in pharmacies.

The métro: clearly marked, clean and efficient

The *Thomas Cook European Timetable* has details of train services, including night trains, and is available to buy from Thomas Cook branches in the UK, *tel: (01733) 416477* or visit *www.thomascookpublishing.com*

Climate

Paris enjoys a temperate climate, with moderate rainfall and a good deal of sunshine in spring, summer and even winter. July and August are hottest, January and February the coldest. The rainiest season is autumn.

Crime

Do not leave anything of value visible in your car. Watch your bag in crowded places. Be particularly careful in areas such as the Forum des Halles, the Gare du Nord and Gare de l'Est districts, including the 18th *arrondissement*, and Strasbourg St-Denis. The métro is safe during the day, but, along with the RER, should be avoided after 11pm.

Driving

Make sure you take your car registration papers and driving licence; an international driving licence is not usually necessary. Your insurance policy covers you for third-party, but if you want comprehensive cover you will need

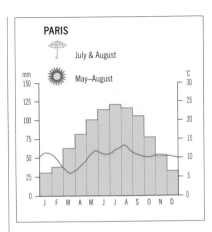

PARIS

July & August

May–August

Weather Conversion Chart
25.4mm = 1 inch
°F = 1.8 x °C + 32

Boules in the Bois de Vincennes

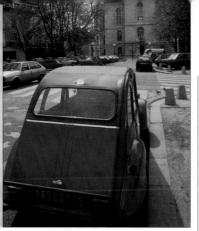

Paris Observatory, centre of research

Conversion Table		
FROM	TO	MULTIPLY BY
Inches	Centimetres	2.54
Feet	Metres	0.3048
Yards	Metres	0.9144
Miles	Kilometres	1.6090
Acres	Hectares	0.4047
Gallons	Litres	4.5460
Ounces	Grams	28.35
Pounds	Grams	453.6
Pounds	Kilograms	0.4536
Tons	Tonnes	1.0160

To convert back, for example from centimetres to inches, divide by the number in the third column.

an International Insurance Certificate (green card). In addition, motoring organisations in your own country have accident/breakdown schemes.

If you hire a car, make sure your domestic insurance covers you for third-party liability; if not, you should obtain top-up cover from your insurers.

Road signs are international. There are four grades of fuel: *gasoil* sometimes spelt *gazolle* (diesel), *super* (98 octane), *sans plomb* (95 octane unleaded) and *super sans plomb* (98 octane unleaded).

A detailed map of Paris which clearly indicates one-way streets is essential. Wearing seat belts is compulsory, and speed is limited to 50kph (31mph) throughout the city, but 80kph (50mph) on the *périphérique*.

The *priorité à droite* (giving way to traffic approaching from the right) is strictly observed and bus lanes should be kept clear.

Parking can be a problem and you may decide to leave your car in a long-term car park (ask at your hotel). In the city centre, there are parking spaces along the kerb marked *payant* and ticket distributors nearby; the maximum time allowed is

Men's Suits

UK		36	38	40	42	44	46	48
Rest of Europe	46	48	50	52	54	56	58
US		36	38	40	42	44	46	48

Dress Sizes

UK		8	10	12	14	16	18
France		36	38	40	42	44	46
Italy		38	40	42	44	46	48
Rest of Europe	34	36	38	40	42	44
US		6	8	10	12	14	16

Men's Shirts

UK	14	14.5	15	15.5	16	16.5	17
Rest of Europe	36	37	38	39/40	41	42	43
US	14	14.5	15	15.5	16	16.5	17

Men's Shoes

UK	7	7.5	8.5	9.5	10.5	11
Rest of Europe	41	42	43	44	45	46
US	8	8.5	9.5	10.5	11.5	12

Women's Shoes

UK	4.5	5	5.5	6	6.5	7
Rest of Europe	38	38	39	39	40	41
US	6	6.5	7	7.5	8	8.5

two hours (traffic wardens are very efficient). However, parking is free almost everywhere during August. There are also underground car parks at Notre-Dame, Hôtel de Ville, Les Halles, Concorde, etc.

All the major international car hire companies are represented in Paris; they operate from a central booking telephone number, but you can pick up a car from various points in the city.
Autorent *Tel: 01 45 54 22 45.*
Avis *Tel: 01 55 38 67 20.*
Europcar *Tel: 01 30 44 93 84.*
Hertz *Tel: 01 47 88 51 51.*
There is also the internet-only car rental company, *www.rentacar.com.* Most of these also offer chauffeur-driven cars.

Electricity
Supply is 220 volts. Two-pin continental plugs can be used everywhere, even in power sockets.

Consulates
Australia *4 rue Jean Rey, 75015.*
Tel: 01 40 59 33 00.
Canada *35 avenue Montaigne, 75008.*
Tel: 01 44 43 29 00.

Be sure to put a valid ticket on your car

Scooters are a popular way to get around

Ireland *4 rue Rude, 75016.*
Tel: 01 44 17 67 00.
New Zealand *7 ter rue Léonard de Vinci, 75016. Tel: 01 45 00 24 11.*
South Africa *59 quai d'Orsay, 75007.*
Tel: 01 53 59 23 23.
UK *35 rue du Faubourg-St-Honoré, 75008. Tel: 01 44 51 31 00.*
US *2 rue Saint Florentin, 75001.*
Tel: 01 43 12 22 22.

Emergency numbers
Police Secours (accidents): *17.*
Pompiers (fire): *18.*
Samu (ambulance): *15 & 01 45 67 50 50.*
SOS Médecins (doctor): *01 47 07 77 77.*
SOS Dentaire (dentist): *01 43 37 51 00* from 9am to midnight.
Burns *01 44 73 62 54* (children), *01 42 34 17 58* (adults).
Poison Centre *01 40 05 48 48.*
Locksmith *01 47 07 99 99.*

Health
EU residents should obtain a European Health Insurance Card (available online at *www.ehic.org.uk*, from the post office or *tel: 0845 606 2030*) before travelling, to enable them to receive the same benefits as French nationals. However, as only 70 to 80 per cent of medical expenses are reimbursed, even with the use of the card, visitors to France are advised to take out a separate medical insurance. For residents outside the EU,

they should obtain the relevant information from their own country.

National holidays

On these days, administrative offices and banks are closed, as well as some monuments and museums. Some shops and hypermarkets remain open.

1 January New Year's Day
Variable Easter Monday
6th Thursday after Easter
Ascension Day
2nd Monday after Ascension Day
Whit Monday
1 May May Day
8 May Victory in Europe Day (1945)
14 July Bastille Day (National Day)
15 August Assumption Day
1 November All Saints' Day
11 November Armistice Day
25 December Christmas Day
Many shops and restaurants are closed during August.

Universal sign of frustration: no entry

Lost and found office

Préfecture de Police, 36 rue
des Morillons, 75015.
Tel: 08 21 00 25 25. Métro: Convention.
Open: Mon–Thur 8.30am–5pm,
Fri 8.30am–4.30pm.
Lost or stolen credit cards
Carte Bleue/VISA *Tel: 08 92 70 57 05*
(costs approx. 0.34 euros/min).
Eurocard/MasterCard
Tel: 01 45 67 84 84.
Diner's Club *Tel: 08 10 31 41 59.*
American Express *Tel: 01 47 77 72 00.*
JCB International *Tel: 01 42 86 06 01.*

Media
Internet
Some useful websites about the city include:
www.parisinfo.com
www.paris-france.org
www.cityvox.com
www.thinkparis.com
http://magicparis.com
www.bonjourparis.com

Newspapers
There are no evening newspapers in Paris. *Le Figaro* and *Le Monde* have supplements or magazines on several days of the week, dealing with cultural events, travelling, books, economic and financial matters, etc.

There is also a profusion of publications containing the weekly radio and TV programmes, with comments and articles on famous people; *Télérama* is one of the best. The whole range of entertainment offered by the capital is reviewed in detail by two very cheap weekly publications, issued on Wednesday – *Pariscope* and *L'Officiel*

LANGUAGE

BASIC WORDS		railway station	la gare
AND PHRASES		**platform**	le quai
yes	oui		
no	non	**NUMBERS AND**	
please	s'il vous plaît	**QUANTITY**	
thank you	merci	**one**	un/une
excuse me	excusez-moi	**two**	deux
I am sorry	pardon	**three**	trois
good morning	bonjour	**four**	quatre
good evening	bonsoir	**five**	cinq
good night	bonne nuit	**six**	six
goodbye	au revoir	**seven**	sept
I have. . .	j'ai...	**eight**	huit
It is. . .	c'est...	**nine**	neuf
Do you speak		**ten**	dix
English?	Parlez-vous anglais?	**a little**	un peu
I do not		**enough**	assez
understand	Je ne comprends pas	**much/many**	beaucoup
when	quand	**too much/many**	trop
yesterday	hier		
today	aujourd'hui	**DAYS OF**	
tomorrow	demain	**THE WEEK**	
at what time. . .?	à quelle heure. . .?	**Monday**	lundi
where is. . .?	où est. . .?	**Tuesday**	mardi
here	ici	**Wednesday**	mercredi
there	là	**Thursday**	jeudi
near	près	**Friday**	vendredi
before	avant	**Saturday**	samedi
in front of	devant	**Sunday**	dimanche
behind	derrière		
opposite	en face de	**MONTHS**	
right	à droite	**January**	janvier
left	à gauche	**February**	février
straight on	tout droit	**March**	mars
car park	un parking	**April**	avril
petrol station	un poste à essence	**May**	mai
parking	stationnement	**June**	juin
prohibited	interdit	**July**	juillet
bridge	le pont	**August**	août
street	la rue	**September**	septembre
bus stop	l'arrêt du bus	**October**	octobre
underground		**November**	novembre
station	la station de métro	**December**	décembre

des Spectacles. Newspapers and magazines are on sale in kiosks dotted about the city as well as in *Maisons de la Presse* (newsagents), *Journaux-Tabacs* (tobacconists) and some bookshops. Most foreign newspapers are available in the centre, at railway stations and airports.

Radio
Apart from the national stations like *France Inter* and *France Culture*, there are many local stations that broadcast on FM for the benefit of the Paris region, from *Radio Classique*, the non-stop classical music programme, to *Nostalgie*, a mixture of French songs and light music, and several ethnic stations.

Television
There are six national channels, four public and two private: *Paris Première* is devoted to Paris and its region.

Money matters
The French currency, as in most of the rest of the EU, is the euro (€). It is divided into 100 cents. There are coins of 1 and 2 euros and of 1, 2, 5, 10, 20 and 50 cents. The notes are of 5, 10, 20, 50 and 100 euros. Exchanging currency (notes, traveller's cheques, credit cards) is no problem in Paris; it can be done in banks all over the city or in bureaux de change.

Traveller's cheques, if denominated in euros, are accepted as cash in hotels, larger restaurants and stores. You can pay by credit card almost everywhere.

If you need to transfer money quickly, you can use the MoneyGram^{SM} Money Transfer service. For more details

telephone Freephone *0800 897198* (in the UK).

Opening times
Banks: *10am–5pm except Saturday, Sunday and holidays.*
Bureaux de change: *6.30am–11pm at airports, 6.30am–10pm at railway stations, 10am–7pm in town.*

If you find yourself short of cash outside the above opening hours, try an ATM. More and more now accept foreign credit cards and have easy-to-follow instructions.

Museums: national museums are closed on Tuesday, except the Musée d'Orsay, the Musée Rodin and Versailles, which are closed on Monday. Opening hours are usually from 9am–6pm.

Paris museums are generally closed on Monday and free on Sunday (except temporary exhibitions). They are usually open from 10am–5.40pm.

Shops: most open weekdays 9am–7pm. Some close noon–2pm, some on Monday morning. Department stores are open daily, except Sunday, from 9.30am–6.30pm, and have a late-closing day midweek. Food shops open at 7am or 8am and close around 8pm; they often close for three hours in the middle of the day. A few also open on Sunday morning.

Organised tours
On foot
The Direction Départementale de la Jeunesse et des Sports de Paris publishes a useful booklet about walks around Paris (*6–8 rue Eugène-*

Oudiné, 75013; tel: 01 40 77 55 00).
Open: Mon–Fri.

By bicycle
Several bicycle-hire companies organise
trips in and around Paris. Contact:
Paris à Velo, c'est Sympa 22 rue
Alphonse Baudin, 75011. Tel: 01 48 87
60 01. Métro: Richard Lenoir.

By bus
Several companies offer tours of the city
and excursions to famous places such as
Versailles and many others.
Cityrama 4 place des Pyramides, 75001.
Tel: 01 44 55 61 00. Métro: Palais-Royal.
Paris Vision 214 rue de Rivoli, 75001.
Tel: 01 42 60 30 01. Métro: Tuileries.
RATP Excursions (run by the Paris
Transport Authority); departure from
place de la Madeleine; for free brochure
and information, tel: 01 40 06 71 45.
Bookings can be done in advance from
place de la Madeleine (métro: Madeleine)
or from 53 bis quai des Grands-Augustins
(métro: St-Michel or Pont-Neuf).

By boat
There are various options for those
wanting to take a cruise on the Seine or
on the Canal St-Martin.
Bateaux Mouches Pont de l'Alma,
75007. Tel: 01 45 25 96 10.
Métro: Pont de l'Alma.
Bateaux Parisiens Pont d'Iéna.
Tel: 01 44 11 33 44.
Métro: Trocadéro, Bir Hakeim.
Vedettes du Pont-Neuf Square du Vert-
Galant, 75001. Tel: 01 46 33 98 38.
Métro: Pont-Neuf.
Canauxrama 13 quai de la Loire, 75019.
Tel: 01 42 39 15 00. Métro: Jaurès.

The bus service is well organised and convenient

Paris-Canal 21 quai de la Loire, 75019.
Tel: 01 42 40 96 97. Métro: Jaurès.
Vedettes de Paris Port de Suffren, 75007.
Tel: 01 44 18 19 50.

Helicopter tours
Exclusive Tours 8 rue du Faubourg
Poissonière, 75010. Tel: 01 42 33 12 51.
Métro: Bonne Nouvelle.

Pharmacies
The following remain open outside
normal hours:
British and American Pharmacy
1 rue Auber, 75009.
Tel: 01 43 35 44 88. Open: daily except
Sunday until 8pm. English spoken.
Métro: Opéra.
Pharmacie Anglaise
62 Champs Elysées, 75008. Tel: 01 43
59 22 52. Open: daily noon–10pm. Métro:
Franklin-Roosevelt.
Pharma Presto
Tel: 01 42 42 42 50. Pharma Presto
operates a 24-hour delivery service
(livraison).

Places of worship
Denominational churches include:
St Michael's Anglican Church 5 rue
d'Aguesseau, 75008. Tel: 01 47 42 70 88.
Métro: Madeleine.

The American Cathedral *23 avenue George V, 75008. Tel: 01 53 23 84 00. Métro: Alma-Marceau.*
St Joseph's Catholic Church *50 avenue Hoche, 75008. Tel: 01 42 27 28 56. Métro: Charles-de-Gaulle-Etoile.*
Church of Scotland *17 rue Bayard, 75008. Tel: 01 48 78 47 94. Métro: Franklin-Roosevelt.*
Synagogue La Victoire *44 rue de la Victoire, 75009. Tel: 01 40 82 26 26. Métro: Notre-Dame-de-Lorette.*
Grande Mosquée *39 rue Geoffroy-Saint-Hilaire, 75005. Tel: 01 45 35 97 33. Métro: Jussieu or Place Monge.*

Police

The **Préfecture de Police** *7 boulevard du Palais 75004. Tel: 01 53 73 53 73.* On the Ile-de-la-Cité is the police headquarters. There are *commissariats de police* (police stations) in each *arrondissement*. **In case of emergency, tel: 17.**

Post offices

Bureaux de poste are open Mon–Fri 8am–7pm, Sat 8am–noon.

The main office (*52 rue du Louvre, 75001; tel: 01 40 28 20 00; métro: Louvre-Rivoli*) is open 24 hours a day, 7 days a week. The address for *poste restante* mail is: *Poste Restante, 52 rue du Louvre, 75001 Paris RP, France.* Stamps can also be bought in a *tabac* (tobacconist). Post boxes are yellow, free-standing, or set into a wall.

Public transport

The métro/RER/suburban railway/buses network is run jointly by the Régie Autonome des Transports Parisiens

A pharmacy located in a lovely old building

(RATP) and the Société Nationale des Chemins de Fer (SNCF). For general information, telephone:
RATP *Tel: 08 92 68 77 14.* English-speaking service, *tel: 08 92 68 41 14.*
SNCF *Tel: 08 36 35 35 35 (6am–10pm).* Passes, available from the main tourist office, métro, RER and railway stations, entitle visitors to use the whole network for one day (*Formule 1*), two, three or five days (*Paris Visite*).

For information about the **Batobus**, *tel: 01 44 11 33 99.* (*Also see p21.*)

Day and night charges are indicated inside taxi cabs; a supplement is due if you board a taxi at a railway station or airport, or have more than one suitcase.

For complaints contact: **Service Taxis, Préfecture de Police**, *36 rue des Morillons, 75015 Paris. Tel: 08 21 00 25 25.*

Senior citizens

Whatever their nationality, senior citizens are allowed a discount in some museums and places of entertainment such as cinemas, on presentation of their passport.

Sport *See pp160–63.*

Allo-Sports (*tel: 01 42 76 54 54; 10.30am–5pm except weekends*) gives information on sports events, clubs and associations.

Student accommodation
Call **Federation Unie des Auberges de Jeunesse** for information (*tel: 01 44 89 87 27; fax: 01 44 89 87 49*). Several youth associations offer cheap lodging: **Ligue Française des Auberges de Jeunesse** Booking systems: *67 rue Vergniaud, 75013. Tel: 01 44 16 78 78.* **CROUS** *39 avenue Georges-Bernanos, 75005. Tel: 01 40 51 55 55.*

Sustainable tourism
Thomas Cook is a strong advocate of ethical and fairly traded tourism and believes that the travel experience should be as good for the places visited as it is for the people who visit them. That's why we firmly support The Travel Foundation, a charity that develops solutions to help improve and protect holiday destinations, their environment, traditions and culture. To find out what you can do to make a positive difference to the places you travel to and the people who live there, please visit *www.thetravelfoundation.org.uk*

Telephones
Calls from hotels are more expensive than from a post office or a telephone booth. Some of these are still coin-operated, but the majority work on a *télécarte* (phonecard) available in post

Outside rush hours, public transport is comfortable

offices, tobacconists and main métro/RER stations.

Numbers in France comprise ten digits. All numbers for Paris and its outskirts begin *01*. There are no area codes. To make an internal call simply dial the number. For the operator dial *13*; for directory enquiries dial *12*.

To make an international call, dial *00* then the country code (Australia *61*, New Zealand *64*, UK *44*, US and Canada *1*), then the area code (minus any initial *0*) followed by the number. It is cheaper to call after 7pm weekdays, or after 2pm Saturday, and all day Sunday.

Time
GMT plus 1 hour (winter), plus 2 hours (summer).

Tipping
Service is included on bills in cafés and restaurants. However, you might want to leave a tip as well. It is customary to tip hotel porters and chambermaids (for a stay of several

days), as well as museum guides, usherettes in cinemas, and taxi drivers.

Toilets

There are public toilets in department stores, cafés and restaurants, and coin-operated booths on the pavements.

Tourist offices

Office du Tourisme et des Congrès de Paris *Carrousel du Louvre, 99 rue de Rivoli, 75001 (tel: 08 92 68 30 00; open: daily 10am–6pm; métro: George V).* There are also branches at all the railway stations, and at the Eiffel Tower. The **Mairie de Paris** has a Bureau d'Accueil at *29 rue de Rivoli, 75004 (tel: 01 42 76 43 43; open: 9am–6pm; closed: Sunday; métro: Hôtel de Ville).*

Travellers with disabilities

Ease of access to sights, museums, theatres and other public places in Paris is improving as the city makes a real effort to welcome visitors with disabilities.

Remember to retrieve your phonecard!

Several brochures on various aspects of daily life are available by mail order directly from local organisations such as: l'Association des Paralysés de France, Délégation de Paris, *17 boulevard Auguste Blanqui, 75013 (tel: 01 40 78 69 00)*, and le Comité National Français de Liaison pour la Réadaptation des Handicapés (CNFLRH), *236 bis rue de Tolbiac, 75013 (tel: 01 45 65 59 00).*

Access in Paris, a fully researched guide for wheelchair users and walkers with disabilities, is available free from Access Projects, *39 Bradley Gardens, London W13 8HE.* It deals with all aspects of travelling to Paris, and how to make the most of it once you are there.

Taxis are not easy to hail, so head for a taxi rank

ACKNOWLEDGEMENTS

Thomas Cook wishes to thank the photographers, picture libraries and other organisations for the loan of the photographs reproduced in this book, to whom copyright in the photographs belongs.

JONATHAN SMITH 9, 10, 12, 13, 14, 19, 24, 28, 30, 31, 40, 46, 48, 52, 54, 64, 66, 67, 68, 69a, 69b, 70, 82, 84, 85, 89, 91, 92, 93, 94, 103, 104, 108a, 108b, 110, 114, 116, 117, 132, 139, 144a, 144b, 146, 151b, 151c, 152, 153, 155b, 157, 158a, 158b, 161, 164, 165, 174, 175, 182; DAVID HENRY 36, 49, 50, 65, 74, 77; PICTURES COLOUR LIBRARY 5, 37, 42, 45, 83, 121, 127, 160; SPECTRUM COLOUR LIBRARY 130; WORLD PICTURES 17, 115

These pictures are held in the AA PHOTO LIBRARY and were taken by ANTHONY SOUTER 2, 27, 34, 35, 43, 44, 51, 60, 61, 90, 99, 101, 105a, 106, 109, 111, 113, 119, 137, 138, 155a, 168, 169, 187b; PHILIP ENTICKNAP 25, 75, 79b; PAUL KENWOOD 88; DAVID NOBLE 124, 125, 126, 128, 129, 135, 141, 143, 172; ERIC MEACHER 166a, 166b, 167a, 167b; and the remaining by KEN PATTERSON.

Copy-editing: PENNY ISAAC

Index: INDEXING SPECIALISTS (UK) LTD

Maps: PC GRAPHICS, SURREY, UK

Proof-reading: JAN McCANN for CAMBRIDGE PUBLISHING MANAGEMENT LTD

Send your thoughts to
books@thomascook.com

We're committed to providing the very best up-to-date information in our travel guides and constantly strive to make them as useful as they can be. You can help us to improve future editions by letting us have your feedback. If you've made a wonderful discovery on your travels that we don't already feature, if you'd like to inform us about recent changes to anything that we do include, or if you simply want to let us know your thoughts about this guidebook and how we can make it even better – we'd love to hear from you.

Send us ideas, discoveries and recommendations today and then look out for your valuable input in the next edition of this title. And, as an extra 'thank you' from Thomas Cook Publishing, you'll be automatically entered into our exciting monthly prize draw.

Emails to the above address, or letters to Travellers Project Editor, Thomas Cook Publishing, PO Box 227, Unit 18, Coningsby Road, Peterborough PE3 8SB, UK.

Please don't forget to let us know which title your feedback refers to!